# TABLE 〔

CHAPTER ONE                                              1
*The Need For a Supply Management Strategy*

CHAPTER TWO                                              9
*Reducing the Supplier Base*

CHAPTER THREE                                           25
*Supplier Certification*

CHAPTER FOUR                                            39
*The Material Positioning Matrix*

CHAPTER FIVE                                            63
*Supplier Selection Strategies*

CHAPTER SIX                                             79
*Strategic Partner Methodology*

CHAPTER SEVEN                                           93
*Typical Supplier Strategies*

CHAPTER EIGHT                                          111
*Global Strategies*

CHAPTER NINE                                           129
*Measurements*

CHAPTER TEN                                            143
*Case Study*

Resource Guide                                         155

Index                                                  159

# HOW TO USE THIS BOOK

This book is designed to be used in conjunction with the corollary texts in our Purchasing Series. Please call us at the number below for more information about utilizing our tools. The idea behind this book is to read it with a pen in your hand so that you can answer the questions and write down the plans you are going to put into action. For those people who use this book alone, there is enough information to get you started on the road to excellence. Remember, however, that roadmaps such as this book are best accompanied by travel guides such as the ones we offer in the field of purchasing. Together, they can make your journey a rewarding one.

## HELP DESK HOTLINE
## 1-800-547-4326

In order to answer the questions of our readers, we have established a Help Desk Hotline at our corporate headquarters in West Palm Beach, Florida. We invite you to call us with your queries about how to use the forms and tools in this book.

We also invite you to use our HELP DESK HOTLINE to find out more about other books we publish, as well as our *Supplier Surveys and Audits Forms* software and a videotape series entitled **Supplier Certification: The Path to Excellence**. In addition to books, software and videotapes, we offer over 80 courses which can be scheduled for intensive, in-house seminars. Call us for details.

# Supplier Strategies

*Charles Goldfeld*

PT Publications, Inc.
3109 45th Street, Suite 100
West Palm Beach, FL 33407-1915
(561) 687-0455

Library of Congress Cataloging in Publication Data
Goldfeld, Charles.   1940-
    Supplier strategies/ Charles Goldfeld.
        p.      cm.
    Includes bibliographical references and index.
    ISBN 0-945456-33-6 (pbk.)
    1. Industrial procurement--United States--Management.
    2. Materials management--United States  I. Title. II. Series.
    HD39.5.G65  1998                          98-38604
    658.7'2--dc21                             CIP

## Dedication:

For my wife, Lynn, without whose support nothing is possible, and without whom nothing is worthwhile.

Thanks to my colleagues at Pro-Tech for all of their valuable input.

And special thanks to Janet, my editor, for her diligent efforts and her extraordinary patience.

**ABOUT THE AUTHOR:** Charles Goldfeld is a Manager with Deloitte & Touche Consulting Group, an international consulting and education firm. As a Senior Consultant with Pro-Tech, a company which provided management consulting and education worldwide, Mr. Goldfeld developed and taught standard courses in Operations, Quality Management, Supplier Certification, Continuous Improvement, MRP, Master Scheduling, and Inventory Management, as well as Oracle education and certification classes. In one of his positions with a division of United Technologies, Mr. Goldfeld was instrumental in leading an Asset Management program which resulted in inventory reductions of 90%. He also headed the procurement improvement team which streamlined and reengineered the procurement process, reduced requisition cycle time, and made the system user friendly to nonprocurement personnel.

Mr. Goldfeld offers over 25 years of experience in Purchasing, Materials, Operations, Planning, Inventory and Systems Management. He has a thorough understanding of procurement, materials and inventory processes and how they support the rest of the business. His background includes both commercial and defense related products. Mr. Goldfeld learned the business from the bottom up starting as an assembler on the factory floor and eventually holding positions as Material Manager, Operations Manager, Planning and Systems Manager, and Senior Program Manager. As a result he has enormous insight into the problems and needs at every level of responsibility.

Mr. Goldfeld is active in APICS, the American Production and Inventory Control Society. He has served as Regional Director of Education and Membership and Chapter Development. He has also served as President of the New Haven Chapter twice. He has spoken at Chapter meetings, Regional Seminars, International Conferences and the First World Congress for P&IC. He is a certified professional (CPIM, CIRM). He is also certified by NAPM, the National Association of Purchasing Management (C.P.M.).

Mr. Goldfeld augmented his years of industry experience with a strong business and financial education. He holds an A.S. in Business Administration from Norwalk Community College, a B.S. in Accounting from Sacred Heart University and an M.B.A. in Finance and International Business from the University of Connecticut. He has also done postgraduate work at the University of Connecticut School of Law.

# THE NEED FOR A SUPPLY MANAGEMENT STRATEGY

# CHAPTER ONE

## Are We at War?

Strategy. The dictionary defines strategy as: 'the science and art of employing the political, economic, psychological, and military forces of a nation or group of nations to afford the maximum support to adopted policies in peace and war.' Quite a mouthful, but easily adapted to our situation in the purchasing world. We can argue whether this is peace or war, but if we think war, we will be considerably more successful. What kind of words does your company's mission statement consist of? Does it contain words like: "Be the best supplier of ...," "Be known as the primary source of ...," "Be the supplier of choice in every market we serve,"?

Beginning to sound a little like a war? We want to be first in every market, to be a leader in our industry. We want to be the company that survives into the next century. How many companies can be number one? How many companies can be first in a marketplace? Only one! Then I have to say we are at war. Not the kind that will use military weapons and not the kind that will physically annihilate our competition, but the kind that says only one of us wins. Only one of us gets to be the best. Only a few of us will really be able to compete in the global marketplace that is fast becoming our arena. Only one of us can be the most efficient producer/provider of goods and services within the shorter product life cycles we are experiencing today.

## Do We Need a Plan?

For your company there is definitely a strategic plan, a road map that it will follow to attain these noble but necessary goals. But what about Purchasing's strategic plan? Does it say anything more than it will support the company's strategic plan?

The purchasing function has long been the focus of blame for everything that goes wrong in a manufacturing facility. The one thing that is always visible is that the parts are not here. No matter what else caused the problem, the fact remains clearly that the parts are not here. We know there were development problems and numerous design changes (both internal and from the customer), and late engineering releases followed by a plethora of engineering changes. We know we lacked enough time in the schedule to properly quote and get the required material. But no one wants to remember all of these contributing factors. Only one simple theme remains, we cannot build the product because we do not have the parts.

I believe that before they were born, while still in their mother's womb, manufacturing managers and supervisors learn the words that will carry them through the rest of their careers. "Get me the parts, and I will build whatever you want." They have always had an excuse for not producing, and we in Purchasing are it. We, of course, have a litany of what we think are acceptable reasons for the material not being there. We can point to the shortcomings of an overzealous, front-end loaded master schedule. We can look at the late engineering releases and point out that the hardest parts to get, which also have the longest lead time, were released last instead of first. We can show that these parts were subsequently changed as the engineers refined (pronounced 'finished') their designs. We can point to the inadequacy of the planning and scheduling departments.

We can point to all of these things, but the real problem is that it is our job to be successful despite all of these things, many of which we believe we will not be able to control. However, if we want to be all things to all people, we better have a supplier strategy that supports that objective. Interestingly enough my latest fortune cookie said 'Hope for the best, but plan for the worst.' The operative word here is *plan*. We will not be the best unless there is a plan in place that will make us the best: a plan that is based on actual facts about the current state of affairs, a plan that clearly defines the goal of where we need to get to, a plan that details the steps required to achieve the desired results.

And not just any plan to get better will do. The objectives we set forth for ourselves in Purchasing/ Procurement need to be based on a clear understanding of our company's strategic plan for the future. Then we need to align our strategies in a way that directly supports the direction our companies are headed in. We must take into account the key factors for our success in the marketplace, measure these against the procurement risk involved in acquiring these materials and then incorporate them into our choice of supplier strategies.

## Where Do We Start?

Any strategy we select will, of course, take time to implement. And as you have already guessed, this will be on top of the mountains of work that already consumes our time. Therefore part of our strategy will have to include not wasting our precious time performing functions that:

1. do not get us any closer to the achievement of our stated goals and

2. can be handled by others and, therefore, do not necessarily require the time and attention of our buyers.

Many of these tasks are related to the acquisition of goods and services that do not affect our success in the marketplace one iota. These may be the procurement of MRO (maintenance repair and operating) supplies, office supplies, nuts, bolts, screws and other items that are plentiful and easy to procure. So spending a lot of time on these activities has little or no return in terms of our true objectives. In fact, they accomplish the opposite. They keep us from reaching our goals by consuming the very resources that we will need so desperately.

So where do we start? **Our goal is to identify** the factors that are key to our success in the marketplace and concentrate our efforts on fine tuning those resources that are critical to that success. And since the resources we are referring to are our suppliers, we should take a moment to think about our approach. There are a number of things that make an awful lot of sense.

1. Reducing the number of suppliers we have in the base

2. Adopting a Supplier Certification Program as a means to achieving the 'partnering' relationships with our most critical suppliers as a way of guaranteeing our success

Once we have reduced our supplier base and begun the process of developing partnering relationships we can concentrate on the balance of our strategic plan. We will then:

1. identify the key factors that influence our success in the marketplace and determine what effect the materials we procure have on that success.

2. assess the procurement risk inherent in the acquisition of those materials.

The combination of these two criteria will help us determine where each of the parts that make up our products fall on the Material Positioning Matrix. Where parts fall gives us the key to our best approach to their procurement by selecting the strategies that have the most chance of success under those circumstances.

## How Will We Measure Our Success?

As we progress along our strategic path it is important that we take some measurements. The first will be to drive a stake in the ground so we understand where we are today. Then we need to establish the goals and objectives that enable us to be successful. The measurements we choose should clearly show our progress against the milestones that were set in the plan. In this way it all ties together. We will have a set of strategies that support the strategic direction of our companies. We will have a plan in place to achieve them. And we will have a methodology in place to measure our results against our milestones to ensure we are achieving our objectives at the desired rate. If we aren't, we should know it in enough time to take whatever corrective action is required.

## The Right Track

We will know we are on the right track when our company begins to think of the purchasing function as a strategic weapon in our war against the competition. When our overall procurement strategies, of which supply management is but one, make us more competitive and successful in our chosen markets, when the rest of the company includes us in their strategic planning because we can help make them more successful by providing the services they will require ... it is then that we can stand back and pat ourselves on the back for achieving our potential. Stand back, but not rest. Now we have to continue to develop the strategies that will keep us in the number one position we aspired to.

# REDUCING THE SUPPLIER BASE

## CHAPTER TWO

## A Bad Assumption

After World War II America experienced a period of economic growth that by all measurements was astounding. Unfortunately, many of us did not understand the underlying causes. The plain fact of the matter was that much of the world was devastated, either physically, from having waged a war on their own soil, or economically, from having poured a tremendous amount of money into supporting the war effort. America had built a tremendous manufacturing capacity which it now turned toward the production of industrial and consumer goods. There was only one real source of supply and that was America.

We made a bad assumption. We made the mistake of attributing our success to our superb management style and efficient manufacturing methodologies. Unfortunately, we missed the point. Essentially, we were the only game in town. In fact, we were successful despite our management styles and methods precisely because we were the only place to come. We were the supplier to the world, and the world was hungry.

This fatal mistake led us to teach these styles in our business schools. We then turned out a generation of managers that continued to support outdated strategies and methods of running companies, including procurement strategies that were counterproductive. Among those were some assumptions about our suppliers and how they should be dealt with.

## A Strange Dichotomy

We have a strange dichotomy at work at many of our companies today. If we are asked the question of whether we have too many suppliers we would probably answer 'yes.' And yet some of us would also say we cannot meet the needs of the companies because we do not have enough suppliers. I suspect what we mean is that we do not have enough of the right suppliers, which can be simply defined as those that meet our requirements. Our requirements can also be very easily defined: not merely as the right material at the right time, but 100% of the material (which means all of it), with 100% quality (which means it is all good and usable), 100% on time (which means when we asked for it/needed it), 100% of the time (which means all of the time).

## Why Do We Need So Many Suppliers?

Whenever the subject of supplier reduction comes up, I usually get the same arguments in support of not reducing the number of suppliers. We need all of our suppliers for some combination of the following reasons.

1. We do not believe in sole-sourcing as a strategy.

2. We cannot afford to be at the mercy of one supplier.

3. I need to split my business so I always have another producer in the wings.

4. We are not a big enough customer for one supplier to carry the variety we need.

5. We have to have at least three quotes before we can commit.

6. We cannot negotiate competitive pricing without competition.

7. Murphy's law says that something will happen.

All of these concerns can be addressed.

1. Sole-sourcing can indeed lead to problems and in many cases would be a poor strategy. When no alternative exists we need to learn how to make the best of it. I prefer instead to use single-sourcing. The fact that there are other sources allows me to choose the best one and favor that supplier with the bulk of my business.

2. I am not at the mercy of one supplier just because I have opted for a single source. In fact the very

reason I chose a single supplier allows me to address the other areas of concerns and find viable solutions for them.

3. Competing suppliers will know up front what it takes to win my business and, therefore, would be waiting in the wings for either the other to fail or an opportunity to enhance their own chances of becoming the single source in the coming years.

4. Giving a single supplier the bulk of my business would allow me to leverage my purchasing power and coax the supplier into handling other required items as part of retaining their single-source position.

5. Three quotes for every item are not necessary. We have even made progress in convincing government agencies that we do not intend to fulfill this requirement. And still we are prepared to show that we have indeed obtained the lowest pricing available for each commodity. We can do this by selecting suppliers whose costs we understand, whom we have examined and found to be the lowest cost producer and with whom we have agreed on what their profit margins ought to be.

6. By competing and negotiating long-term agreements for a variety of goods that are based on agreed upon pricing structures, we can get the best pricing while maintaining competition and single-sourcing.

7. Even though we sometimes think of Murphy as an optimist, things can go wrong when we have

many suppliers, not just one. The key here is planning, planning and more planning. One of the areas we will address later in this book is procurement risk as it relates to each commodity. Here we need to address risks that we know about and should be including these risk factors as part of our selection criteria when choosing the right suppliers.

## Contingency Planning

I would like to spend just a few minutes on risk and contingency planning. I used to work for a CEO who each year sent out a memo that contained just four words: "It snows in December." What he meant by this cryptic message was that in this part of the country it snows in the wintertime. And since we all chose to live and work here, we need to think about its effects on our business.

Storms should be expected and planned for. Delays in transportation should be expected, and perhaps (for a short time only) lead times ought to be increased by a few days. Local plants may shut down. Our own plant may be forced to close because of weather. All of these are not valid excuses for missing any production or purchasing commitments or commitments to our customers. There are 'environmental' factors (not all weather related) around the world that need to be taken into account as we select our suppliers and plan our supply chains.

Contingency plans need to be drawn up and put in place. A very important note is that all of the contingency planning does not have to be ours. As part of our criteria for selecting those suppliers that we intend to partner with we should be reviewing their contingency plans. What do *they* intend to do to combat expected delays because of weather or other natural disasters in their area or in the space that lies between us? Are *they* maintaining excellent working relationships with their labor forces to mitigate against strikes, walkouts and even internal sabotage? Do *they* have other facilities that can handle our parts should their main plants become incapacitated due to fire, earthquake or other unexpected disaster? In short, are they the kinds of companies that care enough about our success that they have plans in place to see that the flow of goods into our plant remains constant and uninterrupted? That takes the burden off us and does not consume any of our resources in the process.

## Benefits of Reducing The Supplier Base

One of the things we all complain about is not having enough time to do all of the things we need to accomplish. Most of us would also say that we probably spend less than 25% of our time doing what we were hired to do. Just think about how much time is being consumed needlessly because our supply base is just too large. Some of the main advantages of reducing the supplier base are listed below. As you review them think of all the time and effort associated with each one.

1. Fewer suppliers to manage means that there is less of all of the things that are necessary to maintain a supply base.

   • Less maintenance of supplier records both on the computer and off

- Fewer annual quality surveys
- Fewer checks to write in Payables
- Fewer accounts to maintain
- Fewer deliveries to receive
- Fewer sales offices to deal with
- Fewer sales reps to see
- Fewer RFQs to be sent out

2. We can leverage our purchasing power because we will be spending more dollars with each of the suppliers that we retain. We also become a more important customer to them as we account for a greater percentage of the suppliers' sales.

3. We can develop closer relationships with our suppliers (the precursor to partnering) simply because we will have more time to spend with fewer suppliers.

4. If we have a problem it should be more easily resolved, because:

   - we will have closer relationships because suppliers will be more knowledgeable about our business.
   - we will be more important to suppliers.
   - we have culled out the poorer suppliers.

## How Big a Reduction Should We Make?

What generally happens is our CEO, CFO, COO or some other member of top management sat next to somebody on a plane who told our executive that at his company they reduced their supplier base by 70% and the benefits have been just fantastic. (This also occurs when we send our leaders to seminars.) So, on the CEO's first day back in the plant, he presents this great idea. "Let's reduce our supplier base by 85% (because we do things bigger and better than everyone else), and then we will get better than fantastic results. And, by the way, there isn't any reason we can't do this in three months, because the sooner we cut out all of these suppliers, the sooner we start getting the better than fantastic results."

Where did the 85% goal come from? Literally out of the air since the CEO was probably at 37,000 feet when he thought it up. Is it cast in concrete? Probably not. It was a decision (or goal) set or made without facts. Can we argue with it? Absolutely not, not until we have facts. Any statements like: 'That's too deep,' 'We are different from the other company,' 'We cannot cut that quickly,' or 'We do not have the staff or the time for a project like this,' will all be viewed in a negative light that says we do not understand the problem … we do not understand the business … we are not team players … we are not professionals … we are not good about keeping up with the latest ideas in our field … we are not forward thinkers. Not a pretty picture, is it? All we meant to do was throw a little caution into the equation, and now we have succeeded in planting the seeds that say we need to be replaced.

The alternative is a plan that is based on facts. If we have the facts then we can support an argument for whatever the right number of suppliers is. And as long as it is based in actual facts, there will usually not be any opposition from the top. Management is interested in the fact that we understand what it takes to accomplish our end of the business utilizing the very latest techniques that make up our profession. A plan that explains why the number should be higher or lower should be accepted without a lot of questions.

Or if we do not have all of the facts, we should have a plan that says here is the way we are going to approach reducing the supply base. These are the steps we are going to take, these are the milestones we will be putting in place, including when we will review the number again, and these are the results that we expect.

## What Is Involved In Reducing The Supplier Base?

To start with: a greater understanding of what our needs are and what the current environment is. This actually comes under the heading of commodity management. Do we know enough about the things we buy to make some intelligent decisions? The good news is that with today's computer systems we should have enough information at our finger tips to answer some very simple questions and gather some relatively simple statistics. This information should allow us to put together a plan that is reasonable in its objectives, its time frame and its chances for success.

Here are two basic tools that should be easy to set up using information that should already be in your database. The first is a breakdown of your commodities. For each commodity we need:

- the part numbers that make up that commodity.
- the number of suppliers from which we currently buy each part.
- the annual dollars spent on each part.
- the annual volume in pieces.
- percentage of the total that this part represents.
- whether or not the part is active.

The computer should be able to sum the columns and also provide the dollar share of each part within each commodity. The chart for this should look something like Figure 2.1.

The second tool starts with the information gathered in the first. Here we add some analysis when completing the chart. For each commodity we will need:

- the number of suppliers that currently supply this commodity.
- the required number of suppliers for this commodity. Here we will want to think about why we buy from some of our suppliers and do we think there are ways to reduce this number, including, but not limited to, asking a preferred supplier to carry some additional items in order to become more of a full service provider.
- the number of suppliers that meet our requirements. Remember our requirements were easily defined as: 100% of the material (which means all

# SUMMARY COMMODITY LISTING

**PURCHASED MATERIAL**
**PER COMMODITY TYPE VALUE/VOLUME**

| Code | Commodity Type | # Of Suppliers | Part # | Usage 12 Months $$ | Volume 12 Months $$ | Share % | Active |
|------|----------------|----------------|--------|--------------------|---------------------|---------|--------|
| 05000 | Semiconductors | | | | | | |
| 10000 | Passive Components | | | | | | |
| 15000 | Electromagnetic Components | | | | | | |
| 20000 | Assemblies | | | | | | |
| 25000 | Distributors | | | | | | |
| 30000 | Cabinets, Racks & Accessories | | | | | | |
| 35000 | Capital Equipment | | | | | | |
| 40000 | Buildings | | | | | | |
| 45000 | Software Products | | | | | | |
| 50000 | Energy | | | | | | |
| 55000 | Office Supplies | | | | | | |
| 60000 | Telephone | | | | | | |
| 65000 | Sheet Metal | | | | | | |
| 70000 | Injection Molding | | | | | | |
| 75000 | Furniture | | | | | | |
| 80000 | Printing Material | | | | | | |
| 85000 | Advertising Supplies | | | | | | |
| Totals | | | | | | | |

*Figure 2.1*

of it), with 100% quality (which means it is all good and usable), 100% on time (which means when we asked for it/needed it), 100% of the time (which means all of the time).

- the required number of new suppliers. The difference between the previous two columns less the number of suppliers that we think we can grow into suppliers that will meet our stated requirements.

- annual dollar volume of purchases within that commodity. This number will have two uses. First, it can help set the priority as to where to place our efforts. Second, it will also be used in negotiations with suppliers when looking to leverage our purchasing power. We should also be looking at suppliers that handle more than one commodity to further increase our leverage.

- the number of part numbers making up that commodity.

- the annual number of piece parts used.

The form for the resulting chart should look like Figure 2.2.

From these two tools we can put together our supplier reduction plan, a plan that we will know is based on facts, is achievable and can be supported (defended, if you will) against any unreasonable goals that may have been set for us.

# SOURCING WORKSHEET

| Commodity | Code | Present No. of Suppliers | Required No. of Suppliers | Suppliers Meeting Req't | Required New Suppliers | Yearly Dollar Volume Purchased | Number of Part Numbers | Twelve Months Usage |
|-----------|------|--------------------------|---------------------------|-------------------------|------------------------|--------------------------------|------------------------|---------------------|
|  |  |  |  |  |  |  |  |  |
|  |  |  |  |  |  |  |  |  |
|  |  |  |  |  |  |  |  |  |
|  |  |  |  |  |  |  |  |  |
|  |  |  |  |  |  |  |  |  |
| Totals |  |  |  |  |  |  |  |  |

*Figure 2.2*

## This is a Company Project.

Contrary to popular belief, reducing the number of suppliers in the supply base is not a Purchasing project. It is a company-wide project that happens to be led by Purchasing, because Purchasing is the major point of contact with each supplier. Remember that the benefits are also company-wide. In order for a reduction to be successful it needs to be supported by a number of areas within the company. And as such the success of the project should be part of the performance evaluations of each of those individuals.

## Steering Committee and Commodity Teams

Any company-wide project requires a steering committee, a cross-functional group of individuals high enough in the company hierarchy to ensure the success of the project. Their purpose is to help set the goals, help select and staff the teams, approve the plans, measure the results, promote the project to others (keep it visible to upper management and to all areas of the company), provide any required education. The steering committee should be made up of all of the associated disciplines that have a vested interest in the size, quality and performance of the supply base. While representatives from Purchasing, Quality, Engineering and Manufacturing are obvious, be sure to include someone from Finance. His/her role will be twofold. First, any project of this size will require funding. It is important that Finance understand the costs as well as the benefits of the project. Second, a representative from Finance is probably the best choice for measuring the project and its success. That way we will not have to argue with them about where the numbers came from. The steering committee should be capable of handling several related projects. For example, there may also be a supplier certification program in the works or perhaps a benchmarking project.

The actual execution of the plan will be relegated to the commodity teams. Each team should consist of a leader (usually the buyer for that commodity) and some interested stakeholders. They include the quality person responsible for that commodity, the primary engineer that designs in that commodity, and the manufacturing supervisor that primarily uses that commodity. Here again, I like to involve some representatives from Finance. It provides another perspective as well as an opportunity for Finance to help us, by becoming part of the solution.

## Goals

Properly implemented, a well defined and executed supplier reduction program should yield significant results. We always like to suggest a 2:1 reduction in one years time. In other words, your goal should be to achieve a 50% reduction. In two to three years, you should be looking for a 5:1 reduction, or 80%. And in four to five years a 10:1 reduction or 90%. My recommendation is always a maximum of two suppliers per part with the ultimate goal of moving to a single supplier per commodity.

For those who believe that the goals stated above are impossible to achieve, I must tell you that they are not.

Every company is different, and their results will be different. The table below in Figure 2.3 shows not only varied results, but also that a substantial reduction in the supplier base is always possible.

## EXAMPLES OF SUPPLIER BASE REDUCTION

| | |
|---|---|
| Allen Bradley | 20% in 2 years |
| Ford | 35% in 3 years |
| Motorola | 40% in 3 years |
| 3M | 64% in 3 years |
| H.P. (Greeley Div.) | 47% in 4 months |
| Xerox | 94% in 4 years |
| Brown & Williamson (MRO Suppliers) | 60% in 18 months |
| Schering Plough | 15% in 1 year |
| ABB | 25% in 2 years |
| Apple Computer | 52% in 1 year |
| XOMED | 25% goal in 1 year |

*Figure 2.3 – From* Power Purchasing: Supply Management in the 21st Century *(PT Publications, West Palm Beach, FL)*

## SUPPLIER CERTIFICATION

## CHAPTER THREE

## Certification - An Overused Term

I hear a lot of talk about certified suppliers. Over the years I have done business with a number of suppliers that had plaques on their walls proclaiming that they were certified suppliers. And, just as soon as I could, I had them removed from my supply base. I have often wondered how they became certified suppliers, finally reaching the conclusion that there are too many definitions for certified suppliers. Companies are handing out certifications like business promotions. The questions that immediately pop into my mind are: Who certified them, and what exactly is the criteria that their certification was based on? We would like to make sure that we do not fall into the same trap. A certified supplier should be certified because they consistently achieve the kind of excellence we will need from our supply base.

## Who Should Be Certified?

Certification should definitely be reserved for excellence. It should communicate to everyone that this company has met the test of a rigorous program of supplier certification, that here is a company that can be depended upon to meet or exceed our expectations, that this company is among the best in the business. Certification should mean that here is a company anybody would be proud to partner with. We will discuss partnering methodology in a later chapter.

## The Goal of Certification

Keeping to our theme that the goal of the procurement function is to give our companies a competitive advantage in the marketplace, what should we be pursuing strategically toward that end? How would we define the suppliers we want to move forward with? The previous chapter talked about reducing the supply base. Logically that means placing more and more faith in fewer and fewer suppliers. Actually it is more than faith we are placing. We will literally be putting our future and our company's future in the hands of a select supply base. The goal of supplier certification then has to be to find and cultivate those suppliers that are not only capable of becoming certified suppliers, but also those willing to join us in our journey. As you will see, the journey is not easy and not cheap. Certification is a long process. It should be clear that the ultimate goal is a mutually beneficial partnership.

## Characteristics of a Certified Supplier

How would we describe a certified supplier? What are the criteria for attaining certification? It would be easy to say that certified suppliers are those that meet our requirements. Remember our requirements were easily defined as: 100% of the material (which means all of it), with 100% quality (which means it is all good and usable), 100% on time (which means when we asked for it/needed it), 100% of the time (which means all of the time). A certified supplier should be much more than that. What are some of the other attributes of a certified supplier?

- **Financially Stable -** Certified suppliers will be financially stable. As we reduce the supplier base, we really need to make sure that those companies that we are working more closely with stay in business. A financially stable company offers us that kind of longevity. It will also mean that there is a high probability that this is a well run company. I say probability, because I have seen many financially stable companies (usually cash rich), that were very poorly run.

- **Quality Management -** Certified suppliers have real quality management. Not a quality department that has a manager, but a management system that supports and drives the quality initiative. When Robert Galvin at Motorola first broke the news to his staff that they were about to go after Six Sigma quality levels (3.2 defects per million), they were doubtful. They explained to him they didn't think they knew how to do it. He told him that he didn't either, but together they would figure it out. They set their goals for a 10 fold improvement each year until they reached Six Sigma levels.

Galvin did not set the goal and then wait for people to report back their successes or failures at some later date. Instead he put quality as the first agenda item for every meeting they held. So, before they talked about profits, sales or any other issues, they talked about quality and customer service, how they were going to achieve Six Sigma, and where they were on their journey. He put in place formal written policies, measurable quality objectives, performance metrics and defined clear lines of authority and responsibility for quality.

- **Quality System Deployed** - Certified suppliers will have their quality systems deployed throughout their operations. Notice I said their *operations*, not just their plants. A fully deployed quality system encompasses all areas of their business. Product quality is only the obvious part. We need quality in planning, engineering design, engineering change control, document control for policies, procedures, work instructions, methods, routings, etc. We need efficiency in planning, purchasing, inventory management, order entry, finance, etc. We need every process in the company (not just the manufacturing ones) to be at peak efficiency.

We need Human Resource policies that support quality objectives and protect the company's investment in its people. We need to make sure that training programs are in place that give the people the skills they will need to be successful. A fully deployed quality system will do that for us.

Quality system deployment is not sending everybody a copy of the quality manual. At Motorola everybody knows what Six Sigma is. No matter where in the company you go, everyone has the same definition. Everyone knows not only how the company plans to achieve these high quality levels but also what their individual roles are in the process.

- **Good Customer Service -** In addition to maintaining that steady stream of quality parts into our factories, certified suppliers generally should be highly rated as a customer service driven company. We face the challenge of measuring that customer service in an objective vs. subjective manner.

- **Emerging Technology -** Certified suppliers should be on the cutting edge of emerging technologies. They know their product better than anyone else. They would also have gotten close enough to our products to know what makes our products tick. I expect them to use that technology to make a better quality, less expensive component. Their R&D dollars ought to be spent on looking for better solutions for our future business needs.

- **Interested In Our Success** - Certified suppliers should have a vested interest in our success. We should be an important part of their future. However, we want to be careful not to make them dependent on us, to ensure that they do not live or die by what we do. We do want them to feel that part of their success will be measured by our success. We do not want their focus to be on what they can get from us, but rather on what they can do to be a better supplier. How can they help make us more competitive in the marketplace as a strategy for their own well-being?

- **Technical Support** - Certified suppliers should be able to assist us in the development of our products, because we should be headed in the same direction. They will be at the leading edge of their technology, and we should reap the benefits of our "partnering" relationship. We should be designing the next generation of our product with the next generation of theirs, before it gets out to the rest of the world. And hopefully by the time it does get out, we will jointly be on the next version or generation. Remember, many of us have a very short product life cycle (as in electronics, computers and communications equipment). In many industries, if we are not the "firstest with the mostest," we will begin to lose market share. Partnering with the technological leaders, therefore, makes sense.

- **Cost Reduction Goals** - Certified suppliers should be actively pursuing cost reduction goals for themselves. It is one thing for us to demand price reductions. It is something different when our suppliers take the initiative to seek out ways to reduce our costs. In many ways we have tried to emulate some of the practices set forth by our friends in Japan.

A few years ago, a major U.S. auto maker demanded cost reductions despite having negotiated contracts in place. A competing Japanese auto maker, in contrast, while after the same cost reductions uses a different strategy. Instead of expecting price increases each year, they have incentivized the cost reductions. A component that sells for $100 this year is negotiated to be $85 next year and $75 the year after. The auto maker will then assist its suppliers in trying to meet that goal. If suppliers get the price below the goal, the auto maker will let them keep most of the additional profits.

The net result is an organized approach to cost reduction and a win-win-win situation. We win because our costs will be reduced; our suppliers win because their profit margins are increased, and our customers win because they get some of those cost savings also, as well as having a better designed, quality product. Because, if we all did our jobs the right way, we reduced cost by eliminating waste and making the manufacturing process more effective.

- **Measures themselves** - Certified suppliers take a proactive role in measuring themselves. They do not wait for us to come in and tell them that their on-time delivery rate is only 75%, or that their lot acceptance rate is not at the level we expect (if we are foolish to continue to inspect everything that walks in the door). They can tell us what their numbers are, where they were, where they are going and how and when they are going to get there. Their goals are aligned with ours.

- **An efficient producer** - Certified suppliers that have all of the above are well on their way to becoming the most efficient producers that they can be. It makes sourcing a whole lot easier for us. We will know their cost structures, and we will know their profit margins. We can easily determine what a fair price will be. We will also know that any of their competition would be hard pressed to beat their prices and their services. We can, therefore, achieve our goal of single-sourcing, without having to sacrifice competitive pricing.

- **Shorter lead times** - Certified suppliers can deliver in less time than those suppliers that have not worked at being the most efficient supplier they can be. In order to attain the quality levels required, they will have had to fine tune their processes (manufacturing processes included). They will have learned how to produce small quantities (perhaps even one at a time) where feasible, and, therefore, can deliver more quickly than anyone else, without having to keep it on the shelf, in case we order it. Remember, inventory is one of the signs of waste. We will pay the cost of having inventory anywhere in the system. The fact that inventory exists means that the cost will be ours directly or indirectly. Suppliers who want to stay in business have no choice but to cover their costs.

# WIIFM?

Before we begin talking about the process, we ought to ask ourselves, Why would a supplier want to do this? As a supplier, WIIFM comes to mind. "What's in it for me? Why would I want to subject myself to the kind of scrutiny that you are going to put me through? Why do I want to let you get into my books? understand my cost structures? look at my profit margins? examine my systems? review my policies and procedures? share my proprietary technologies? This really has to be good for me, also, or I'm not doing it. Let's take a look at the benefits. I have a lot to gain from this. It will assist me in becoming a more cost-efficient provider." The world has changed. It is much more competitive than it used to be.

Pricing was easy before we had all this competition. If I wanted to make $25 in profit, I merely added $25 to my cost. So if my product cost was $100 my sell price would be $125. If my costs were to rise to $110, my sell price would rise to $135. With the intense competition in today's marketplace, the formula works quite differently. Now my sell price is what the market will bear. If the market will only bear a sell price of $110, and I want to make a profit of $25, I had better figure out how to get my product cost down to $85. Since, on average today, the material content of most products is above 60% and the labor content is down around 12%, where is my opportunity? I need to be the lowest cost, most efficient producer. And in order to accomplish that my suppliers need to also be the lowest cost, most efficient suppliers. Our goals are relatively similar, and we can help each other. So, if my suppliers don't already know it, here is what is in it for them.

## Benefits of Certification to the Supplier

- **More business:**

  - **A much greater share of my current business -** Since I am heading toward a reduced supplier base and single-sourcing, the surviving suppliers get larger pieces of the pie. (This should also give me a price advantage.)

  - **First crack at any future business -** Where will I source my future requirements for new products? Since I have worked very hard on cultivating my certified suppliers and shared with them my vision of the future, it is no coincidence that they would get first crack at my developing products.

  - **More business from the marketplace -** Working with my certified suppliers to make them more efficient producers also has the effect of making them more competitive in the marketplace. They will be able to compete more effectively than ever before. This also allows the suppliers to keep us from becoming their major source of demand, which would force them into a position that would cause them to live or die by the whims of a controlling customer. It will keep us from mistreating them just because we can. We have all seen what happens when a company becomes dependent on us as their sole or dominant customer. We take advantage of them and ask them to do things that we would not like to do.

- **Predictability** - Most of our suppliers are not sitting by the phone like the "Maytag Repairman" hoping we will call. They have a business to run and will be running it. We may be significant customers, but they do not know what we are going to do to them and when we are going to do it. It is like waiting for the other shoe to drop. They will jump through hoops to do what we need them to do, but there is a price. And we will eventually pay for it. As their costs go up due to last minute changes, overtime, expedited deliveries, and premiums to their suppliers, they really have no choice but to pass that on to us.

  But, if suppliers know what our schedules are (and also what they are dependent on), they can schedule their shop around our needs and not make promises to their other customers that they are going to have to break. They can also more effectively smooth out their own production peaks and valleys, getting away from overtime periods followed by periods with furloughs.

- **Support:**

  - **Technical support** - While suppliers are the true experts in what they produce, we as a larger organization can offer technical support in the development of new products that will support our future business. We can offer technical support in the development and improvement of some of their processes.

- **Business support** - A Japanese auto maker, in recognizing that 80% of the materials that go into its automobiles is purchased, has as part of its partnering program an executive loan program. If your CFO, for example, left your company and you were an important supplier to this auto maker, it would lend you someone to be your CFO in order to keep your business up and running and supplying that continuous stream of quality materials into its plants.

- **Educational and training support** - In order to assist in the process of developing our suppliers into the most cost-effective, efficient producers, we should be willing to invest in that strategy. We can accomplish this by training our suppliers in statistical process control, materials management, supply base management and any other topic that will assist them in their journey to excellence.

- **Enhanced communication between our companies** - Having reduced the supplier base we will be able to spend more time with our suppliers as they become a more important part of our business. Communications should be more frequent and clearer than ever before. In fact we may be giving them access directly into our computer systems. The more they know about us and our needs, the better they will able to plan to meet those needs.

- **Leverage their certification** - There are two ways that our suppliers will be able to leverage their certification. First, they should be able to take the results of our surveys and show prospective clients that they have a quality-oriented program already in place. And second, their procedures will have been upgraded during the process which will put them into a position where they can withstand the kind of scrutiny that is becoming part of the standard operating procedures today.

- **Improved payment terms** - If we are getting extraordinary service, plus 100% quality material, 100% on time, 100% of the time, isn't that worth something to us. Imagine not having to expedite, not having to inspect, not having to rework and not having to worry. Just think about being able to sleep peacefully knowing that our certified suppliers will deliver that key material on time as they always do. That has got to be worth something special to us, like paying them on time. What a novel idea!! But that is why I suggested that we add representatives from Finance to our teams. Then they get to see, first hand, that the savings more than justify the early payment.

# THE MATERIAL POSITIONING MATRIX

## CHAPTER FOUR

## Key to Success

The key to devising a successful supply management strategy is to make sure that we have aligned it with our overall company strategy. It is extremely critical that we select a strategy for our supply base that allows us to meet all of our market requirements, those we have today and those we expect to have in the future. Positioning ourselves for today's marketplace alone would be shortsighted, foolish and a waste of time, because by the time we finished we would be in tomorrow's marketplace with today's positioning. So we want to factor into our thinking how we expect our markets to change. We need to be ready to act when our products succeed in the marketplace for different reasons. For example, today we produce the most technologically advanced widget, so our competitive edge is technology. However, as time passes and other companies catch up on the technology, it may be cost or quality that will determine our competitive edge. We need to recognize where our markets are going and have a strategy in place that gets us there, ready to compete by offering the best alternatives.

## Material Positioning

All too often companies leap right into sourcing suppliers, services or materials without taking the time to develop a strategic plan. There are some tools that can help you develop a more proactive process toward supply management. Material positioning tools show how to make supply management more useful and friendly on a day-to-day basis, as they can help us in choosing effective supply strategies. The tools are based upon the recognition that two of the most important factors which determine supply strategy are:

1. the influence on company results.

2. procurement risks.

It is immensely important that we understand our markets and the reasons we are successful in those markets. It is vital that we understand the influence our materials have on those critical success factors and, equally important, the level of procurement risk that is involved in the acquisition of materials deemed to be critical to our success in the marketplace.

## What Do We Have To Do?

There are a number of steps we need to take to develop a supply management strategy.

**A.** Select a cross-functional team for the positioning process.

**B.** Select the material or commodity to be positioned.

**C.** Determine the influence and relative weight on company results.

   1. Determine the elements of market success.

   2. Weight the elements relative to market success.

   3. Calculate the influence on company results.

**D.** Calculate procurement risk.

Determine the relative strength of the competitive forces.

   1. Bargaining power

   2. Rivalry

   3. Substitution

   4. Barriers

**E.** Position the commodity on the positioning matrix.

**F.** Select the appropriate strategies.

**G.** For selected components (strategic at a minimum) assign a cross-functional commodity team.

**H.** Formulate a plan and implement the selected strategies.

## The Material Positioning Matrix

The Material Positioning Matrix shown in Figure 4.1 is where we will plot the results of Steps C and D. The grid allows us to objectively position each commodity we purchase and tell us what type of component we are dealing with. The process by which we determine where an item falls on the grid is managed by a cross-functional team. It is expected that we will have consensus on the criteria, the rankings and, therefore, the results. The ranking process should remove any of the subjectivity that we normally see. We should have definite agreement as to the final ranking and, therefore, agreement on the strategies that will be selected. And since we are talking about the identification of mission critical parts, we will also be in agreement as to which items go first.

Balancing the two elements *Procurement Risk* and *Influence on Company Results* helps set our priorities. There are four quadrants on the grid, representing the four classifications for components of our commodities to fall into.

- **Noncritical Components** - Rankings that fall in the lower left hand quadrant are typically noncritical components. They have little or no influence on company results and they have little or no procurement risk. Our goals and strategies for these components will definitely be different from those for the other quadrants.

- **Leverage Components** - Components falling into the upper left-hand quadrant definitely have an influence on company results, but they too,

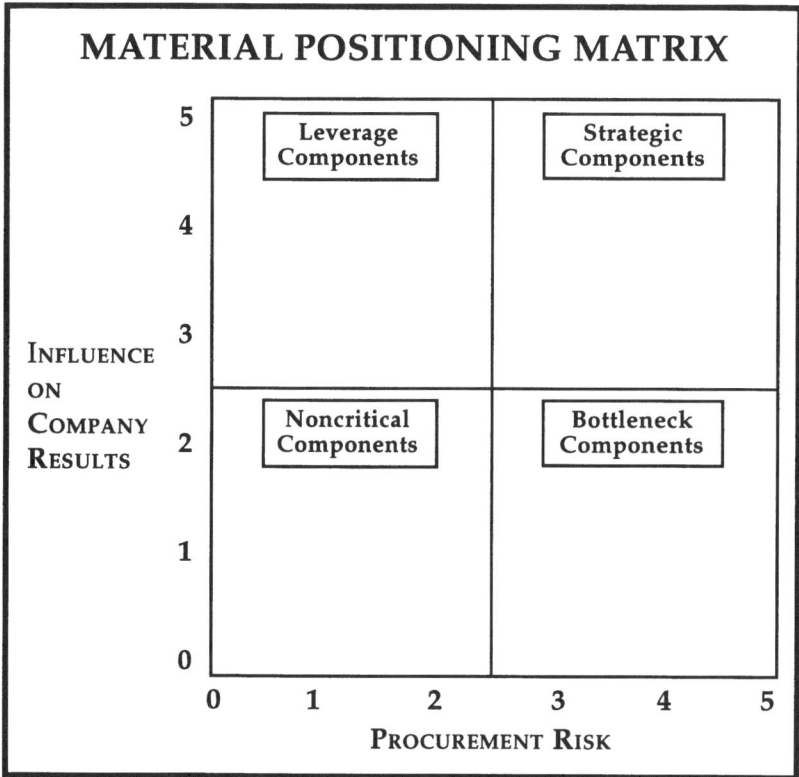

## MATERIAL POSITIONING MATRIX

| | | | |
|---|---|---|---|
| | **Leverage Components** | **Strategic Components** | |
| | **Noncritical Components** | **Bottleneck Components** | |

INFLUENCE ON COMPANY RESULTS

5
4
3
2
1
0

0   1   2   3   4   5

PROCUREMENT RISK

*Figure 4.1*

pose little or no procurement risk. These components are important to us, but they are not difficult to acquire. Our strategy will be different than for noncritical components, but not as severe as those components that will fall in the upper right-hand quadrant.

- **Bottleneck Components** - Components in the lower right-hand quadrant are bottleneck components. They have little or no influence on our success but they do have a greater than normal degree of procurement risk. They are difficult to get, may cause scheduling problems and are usually more trouble than they are worth, because they consume an inordinate share of valuable resources, as well as creating problems and delays, without any real pay back.

- **Strategic Components** - The components that fall into the upper right-hand quadrant have both characteristics. Commodities here play a significant role in our success in the marketplace and also pose problems in their acquisition. If it wasn't clear before, these are our mission critical parts. These are the items that make up that subset of parts that are the primary basis for our competitive edge. These are the items that we want to spend the bulk of our efforts on.

## Overlapping Quadrants

It is important to point out that the quadrants are large and also that we are not taking a precision measurement out to six decimal places. Assuming the coordinates of the midpoint of the matrix are at 2.5,2.5 how much difference is there between parts that plot 2.4,2.4 and parts that plot 2.6,2.6. Yet one of those parts will fall into the noncritical components quadrant, and the other one falls into the strategic components quadrant. Therefore, we should be looking at very similar strategies for both of these components. The one question that always sticks out in my mind whenever I look at the results of a calculation or the outcome of a decision process is: "Does this make sense?" We cannot accept an answer blindly. If we intuitively know that the answer has to be wrong then we want make sure we understood the process we went through to get there. So, if we always operate with "a fanatical application of common sense," we should be successful.

## Determining the Influence on Company Results

There are four factors that affect our success in the marketplace.

- Cost
- Quality
- Time
- Technology

Our products outsell our competitors as a result of one or more of these factors. Our job is to determine for each of our products how each of the commodities we purchase affect our success in our markets. It is easy to lump them together and say we need all of them, and that would be true. Everyone is looking for items that have great quality, the latest technology, instant availability and are inexpensive. We are looking for what differentiates us. It may be that in any given segment of the marketplace, an item may not survive unless it has high quality. Therefore, everybody needs to have a high quality product, and that is not necessarily our competitive edge. Unless we have a higher quality than the competition, we do not have an advantage. Therefore quality would get a lower rating because it would not be the differentiator. That doesn't mean we can produce a shoddy product, it only means that our quality is not the motivating factor in the marketplace.

## A. The Cross-Functional Team

The first step is to select the cross-functional team that will work the positioning process. It is cross-functional for a number of reasons.

1. We want to have as much perspective on the product, the reasons for its success in the marketplace as well as the influence of the commodity as we can possibly get.

2. Once we decide on the strategies to implement, some of the strategies will require cross-functional teams to execute them as well as an investment. The members of this team should be providing the funds and the staffing for the commodity teams that will implement the selected strategies.

3. We get buy-in from the other functional areas that we have selected the right material or commodities to work on, and we eliminate a lot of second guessing or Monday morning quarterbacking that invariably comes from those areas of the business that were not part of the process to begin with.

4. Making sure we include Finance in the team assures us that we will not have to spend a lot of time defending the numbers later. I always ask Finance to provide all the numbers I am going to use. When looking at things like the cost of carrying inventory, the cost of a purchase order, the cost

of an engineering change, and the cost of changing a purchase order, it is very hard to get people to agree on what these numbers ought to be. Arguing about the numbers keeps us from addressing the problems. Therefore, I ask Finance to provide the number so I don't lose the battle of the numbers and miss out on an opportunity to solve a real problem. For example, assume we have an average of five million dollars of inventory in excess of current near term requirements. Do we want to spend our time arguing over whether it costs 10%, 20%, or 30% to carry it? I don't think so. We want to spend our time doing something about it.

## B.  The Targeted Products and Material/Commodities

The second step is to select the products and the materials or commodities that we are going to apply this process to.

1.  The products are relatively easy to do. From our strategic plan we should be able to extract the product(s) that will make or break our future. This is where we will start. Selecting a product that is at the end of its life cycle buys us absolutely nothing. By the time we make a significant impact that product will no longer have as great an effect on our profitability or our position in the marketplace.

2.  Selecting the material and/or commodities is usually just as easy to accomplish. We have a cross-functional team, including Engineering, Marketing or Sales, Quality, Manufacturing and

## INFLUENCE ON COMPANY RESULTS

MATERIAL/COMMODITY _____

| | A<br>Market<br>Success<br>Relative<br>Weight | B<br>Influence<br>of Material<br>(Scale 0-5) | C<br>Weighted<br>Influence<br>(A x B) |
|---|---|---|---|
| **COST**<br>World Pricing<br>Domestic Pricing<br>Cost of Inventory<br>Activity Based Costing<br>Total Cost Management<br>Etc. | _____ | _____ | _____ |
| **QUALITY**<br>Product Quality<br>Service Quality<br>Reliability<br>Etc. | _____ | _____ | _____ |
| **TIME**<br>Long-term Agreements<br>Flexibility<br>Short Lead Times<br>Freight Terms<br>Etc. | _____ | _____ | _____ |
| **TECHNOLOGY**<br>Commodity Leader<br>Equipment<br>Processes<br>Innovations<br>Vision (Future)<br>Etc. | _____ | _____ | _____ |
| **Total** | **1.0** _____ | **Sum of C's** _____<br>**= Influence<br>Index** _____ | |

*Figure 4.2*

Purchasing. These people really ought to know what makes a difference to the customer and what materials and/or commodities are associated with that difference

## C.   The Elements Of Market Success

The third step is to look at our product and determine the relative weight of each of the four factors as determined by our market. (Before we are finished we will do this for each of our products). As with the product we want to also be sure that we are looking at which market we will be in and what the success factors will be. For example, we may be having success today because we have an edge in technology. But if the rest of the world is expected to catch up quickly, then we ought to actually be evaluating what the future success factor is expected to be.

Taking into account the form in Figure 4.2, the numbers we put into Column A are for the product we have chosen. The numbers we will be putting into Column B are for the material or commodity that we are evaluating. The value for each of the factors in Column A (Market Success Relative Weight) will be a decimal such that the sum of the weights will be equal to 1.0. The values in Column B (Influence of Material) are measured on a scale of 0-5. These numbers are not mutually exclusive, a score may be repeated more than once in each of the categories. Again I want to caution you from making everything a 5. Doing so would force the component into the strategic quadrant. Since our goal is to cull out the significant few commodities that we want to concentrate on, making them all 5s would defeat that purpose. The values in Column C (Weighted Influence) are the result of Column A multiplied by Column B.

- **Column A: Market Success Relative Weight**

   Since the values in Column A have to add up to 1.0, we will attack Column A first. Remember, that Column A refers to our product and its success in the market.

   - **Cost** is first element to examine. For Column A we want to understand if cost is our differentiator in the marketplace. In this case we are talking about the selling price of our product. Does our product sell because it is the lowest price? If it is and that is the sole reason, then we would award cost a value of 1.0 and all of the others a value of 0. Conversely, if price is no object then we would place a value of 0 and save our points for the elements that truly make a difference for us.

   - **Quality** is the second element to examine for its effect on our success. When we think about quality, we want to think about all aspects of quality. Not only the quality of the product itself, which includes reliability, serviceability and product life, but also the quality of the service and support we provide. That would include our warranty, our operating manuals, the ease of replacement in case of a problem, access to knowledgeable troubleshooting support, as well as the ease of obtaining access to those services.

– **Time** is the third possible differentiator. How long does the customer have to wait for our product? If it is off the shelf and always in stock and so is our competitors, there is no difference. But if our product is successful because we can consistently beat the delivery times of our competitors, then we have an edge. We should be sure to include in our thought processes our ability to be flexible and deal with customer requested changes within the same short time frames.

– **Technology** is the last element. If we have technology that no one else has or will be able to have (because of patented designs, processes or equipment) we have a clear advantage.

It is important to note that this assessment should not be difficult to make. If in fact our strategic plans were based on good market research, we should already know the answers to these questions. Again, we are moving in the direction of aligning our material strategies with our company's strategic plans.

• **Column B: Influence of Material**

Here we will examine the material or commodity for its effect on the differentiators of our products. The values in Column B relate to the material being assessed.

– **Cost.** If we determined in Column A that cost is a differentiator, then here we are looking at whether this material is a cost driver or not. If cost was not a differentiator, focusing our efforts on reducing the price of this material will have little effect on our success in the marketplace. Then we would award this part a value of 0. Note that it may still have an effect on our bottom line. And we should always be looking at reducing our costs, but in terms of a strategic component this, then, would not be one. If cost is a differentiator for this product and this material is a major cost driver, then we would award it a value of 5.

- **Quality.** Is our quality what makes the difference? If not, focusing on increasing the quality of this item bears no payback in the marketplace. Therefore, a 0 or other low number is assigned. Again, we should not ignore the quality of an item, but for this exercise it will not be important. Should we have a quality program? Absolutely, yes. Should we be looking at increasing our quality levels across the board? Absolutely, yes. We have to do these things to stay competitive anyway.

- **Time.** If time is a differentiator, we would award this item a high number. And then from a strategic standpoint we want to look at what we can possibly do to reduce the amount of time that our customers will have to wait for our product. If time isn't a differentiator, it gets a low value.

- **Technology.** Is this item a key contributor to our technology edge? If yes, then it gets a high value. If not, a low value.

- **Column C: Weighted Influence**

  Column C is the product of Column A and Column B. Since the values in Column A are decimals that add up to 1.0 and the values in Column B are whole numbers from 0 to 5 the sum of the numbers in Column C (The Weighted Influence) will be a number between 0 and 5. The resulting value will plot against the y-axis (Influence On Company Results).

## D.  Calculating Procurement Risk

The fourth step in our process is evaluating how much procurement risk is involved in the acquisition of the targeted material. We do this by examining the relative weight of each of the four elements that make up the competitive forces. Using Figure 4.3, we will rate each of them on a scale of 0 to 5 to determine, for example, when looking at bargaining power, who has the advantage? the buyer or the seller? If the seller has a clear advantage, there is procurement risk. If the buyer has the advantage, the risk is mitigated.

We will then sum the four risks and divide by four which will give us a number (for Procurement Risk) from 0 to 5. This then is the x-axis component of the plot which determines which quadrant the targeted material falls into.

- **Bargaining Power.** The scale runs from 0 to 5. If the buyer has the bargaining power, the score will be 0. If the seller has the bargaining power, the score will be 5. And, obviously, if the balance of the bargaining power is somewhere in the middle, the score will be also.

## PROCUREMENT RISK

MATERIAL /COMMODITY _____

Procurement
Risk
(Scale 0-5)

**BARGAINING POWER**

_____     buyer             seller     _____
_____     0   1   2   3   4   5
_____

**SUBSTITUTION**

_____     easy            difficult    _____
_____     0   1   2   3   4   5
_____

**RIVALRY**

_____     intense           mild       _____
_____     0   1   2   3   4   5
_____

**BARRIERS**

_____     weak             strong      _____
_____     0   1   2   3   4   5
_____

                                          _____
                        SUM/4 =           _____
                                          RISK
                                          INDEX

*Figure 4.3*

Circumstances that give the buyer bargaining power are things like volume purchases (where the buyer is a significant part of the seller's business), standard products that have little or no differentiation between suppliers and are also readily available from other suppliers, and low switching costs (which means it is relatively easy for us to switch suppliers and also relatively easy for us to even switch materials). It also might be just as possible for us to make it ourselves if necessary. This possibility of backward integration becomes another threat to the supplier giving us the bargaining power.

Circumstances that give the seller the bargaining power include a monopolistic or oligopolistic market, where the supplier is the only source or one of the few suppliers of this material, an important or critical product for us. High switching costs, which means it is not easy for us to switch suppliers or materials, also give the seller bargaining power. Does the supplier have the potential for forward integration, i.e., could he incorporate this material into the next higher assembly or end item and become a competitor? Or is the product highly complex as well as being unique to this supplier (a high degree of differentiation)? Again these shift the bargaining power to the seller.

**Substitution.** We want to carefully (i.e., realistically) examine the costs of switching to another material. Coupled with the ability to switch is the realization that there must also be a willingness to switch. Also incorporated into this analysis will be the level of differentiation that exists and how necessary it is. For example, the fact that it is different may not make any difference to the product whatsoever.

– **Rivalry.** Here we are measuring what the competition looks like and where it is going. Is this a growth industry such that we are expecting more and more suppliers to enter the game? If so, the procurement risk is low. If this material or product is in the last stages of its life cycle or in a declining industry, we are likely to experience a shrinking list of suppliers, and the procurement risk increases as time moves forward.

– **Barriers.** What are the barriers for entering this market? Are they high or low? If this product requires a very high level of capitalization (such as the semiconductor industry), it is highly unlikely that we or anyone else will set up a rival business any time soon. Are the required raw materials readily available? Has our government made it very difficult for anyone to enter this market? Are there patents that would keep us from entering? Is the technology one that requires very specialized, scarce and expensive skills? Should anybody enter this market area, how difficult is access to the required distribution network?

The values are now summed and divided by four to get the average procurement risk associated with the acquisition of the material.

## E. Position the Commodity on the Material Positioning Matrix

- The value we attained as the Weighted Influence, or Influence Index, is the Y component (Influence on Company Results) and the value we attained for the Risk Index is the X component (Procurement Risk). The resulting plot gives us the type of component it is and leads us to select the appropriate strategies relative to its acquisition.

## F. Select the Appropriate Strategies

- Experience over time has led us to recognize which of the typical strategies works best for each type of component. See Figure 4.4.
- There are a couple of things to note:
  - Remember that the closer we get to the other quadrants the more similarity there will be in our approach, such that the strength of the indices will help us select.
  - We may want to use a combination of strategies to effectively manage the risk.
  - We may want to use a strategy that doesn't fall into our quadrant or doesn't normally work for this type of component. Since each situation is different, remember the "fanatical application of common sense." The strategies selected have to make sense. Circumstances may dictate the use of a different strategy, which is the reason for the next step.

## STRATEGY MATRIX

| | STRATEGIC | LEVERAGE | BOTTLENECK | NONCRITICAL |
|---|---|---|---|---|
| Partner/Alliance | X | | | |
| Cultivating Suppliers | X | X | X | |
| Long-Term Agreement/Contract | X | X | X | X |
| Standardize | X | X | X | X |
| Quality Improvement | X | X | | |
| Overhead Cost Reduction | X | X | | X |
| Consolidate With Other Divisions | | X | | X |
| Competitive Bidding | | X | | X |
| Price Rollback | | X | | X |
| Supplier Reduction | | X | | X |
| Cross Commodity Leveraging | | X | X | X |
| Internal Price Benchmarking | | X | X | X |
| Re-source to New Suppliers | | | X | |
| Substitute | | | X | |

*Figure 4.4.*

## G. For Selected Components (Strategic at a Minimum) Assign a Cross-functional Commodity Team

- By now you will have come to the conclusion that this is not strictly a Purchasing project, that more than one functional area has a stake in the success of aligning supplier strategies with the company's strategic plan.

- Each mission critical material, commodity or component should be assigned to a cross-functional commodity team for the selection and subsequent deployment of the selected strategies.

- Each team should have a leader, preferably the buyer that buys that material. I always like to see Purchasing take the lead, but if there is a better leader in the group, by all means take advantage of it. The balance of the team should be made up of the following people: the Design Engineer who designed the material into the product and would therefore be responsible for the use of that material in follow-on versions of the product; the Quality Engineer responsible for the quality of the product, as well as the material that goes into it; someone from Manufacturing who is responsible for the part in the manufacturing process; someone from Planning responsible for the product that uses this material and also possibly the material plan that acquires the material; and someone from Finance to make sure that we do not have any trouble with any of the numbers. Again, I always want Finance to be part of the solution instead of part of the group that argues about the numbers, the savings, the benefits, etc. I would even like to have someone from Marketing, if it makes sense to have the representative, who can contribute a different perspective (a customer focus).

- All of these people will add buy-in from the other functional areas they represent. They will add additional resources to the team that Purchasing alone would not be able to support. They will be immensely useful during the supplier surveys, during which we will look at more than just the actual manufacture of the material. We will be examining all of their processes as we look to select the most reliable and efficient suppliers.

## H.    Formulate a Plan and Implement the Selected Strategies

- Each cross-functional team should now put together a plan they can follow to implement the selected strategies for the selected materials.

- Each plan should be a step-by-step approach with assigned responsibilities and measurable milestones so that progress can be measured. Each member of the team needs to know exactly what is expected of him or her and when. We need to be careful to divide up the work equally so that we can all contribute to accomplishing each strategy as quickly as possible. Tasks need not be functionalized or stovepiped. The object is to get the strategies implemented and not worry if a particular task is normally a Purchasing task or a Quality task.

If there are savings expected with the completion of a strategy, we need to make sure that there are baseline measurements in place to compare against. Note that any expected benefits should be in the plans.

# SUPPLIER SELECTION STRATEGIES

## CHAPTER FIVE

Before we begin the process of determining which strategy to use with a particular supplier, we ought to agree on the criteria to be used in the supplier selection process. Remember, since we will be using cross-functional commodity teams in many areas, it is important that we all use the same jargon and agree on the definitions of the relevant terms. This will not only preclude any arguments later on, but will also give us an objective methodology for comparing suppliers.

The methodology we will eventually use will be to assign point values for each of the areas that we will have deemed a critical supplier requirement, which will also be dependent on the commodity. Having agreed on the definition of each of the terms, we will then agree on the number of points to be awarded for each element of the requirement. Again, bear in mind we will determine the values based on what we feel is important to us. For example, we may decide when determining point values for quality management, that we will award considerably more points to a supplier that uses customer satisfaction studies as part of its strategic quality planning than we would for them being ISO 9000 certified. This is primarily because strategic quality planning means there will be improvement goals and plans, whereas ISO 9000 certification is only a measure of consistency and maintaining the status quo.

## A Note of Caution

We need to be careful about how we allow the points to be awarded. Let me give you an example of a good thought gone awry. In one of the companies I worked with we were looking for a Director of Materials. Our Director of Human Resources had done some advertising in local and national newspapers as well as placed a listing on the corporate web site. The response was tremendous, and he received an extraordinarily large number of resumes. The volume was not only far greater than expected, but also much larger than the professional staff could evaluate.

Undaunted, the HR Director devised a point-rating system after sitting down with a few key directors and determining what the qualifications of the successful candidate would be. Points were awarded for degrees and advanced degrees, business experience, subject knowledge, positions held, etc. He then had a number of clerks sift through the resumes, awarding points based on the ratings he had devised. Anyone that scored more than 100 points would be brought in for an interview. As acting Director of Materials I reviewed the selected resumes. I was shocked that there were so many unsuitable candidates in the selected lot.

I then reviewed the point-rating system and found the answer. Because the HR Director was not clear that there had to be a certain number of points from mandatory categories, it was possible to score 100 points without ever having worked a day in Purchasing, Materials Management or Contracting. For us, this means we have to make certain that when we devise our point-rating systems we are careful to ensure that a supplier cannot earn enough points to be selected without having met those requirements that we have deemed critical. There may also be a certain minimum number of categories in which a supplier must rate at acceptable levels in order to be considered.

## Definitions of Supplier Selection Criteria

We will eventually break each of these categories down into their respective elements. Then we will determine exactly how the points are to be awarded. The degree to which we use these definitions will be determined by where in the Material Positioning Matrix each commodity falls and which strategy(s) we have chosen to pursue. Obviously, if we are looking at low cost, low risk items that we will buy from distributors with annual contracts, statistical process control on the factory floor will not be of importance, whereas distribution process control will be a major concern.

Many of the criteria are common across industries, though each of us will have to tailor a checklist that suits our business and the commodities that are important to our success. Let's go through the definitions so we have a common basis from which to move forward. The following are not listed in any particular order, as their relative importance will be different for each of us.

**Distribution Process Control.** The suppliers' distribution processes are well managed, measured and properly controlled. Systems are in place that make sure each customer receives exactly the products that he ordered, in the exact quantities asked for (no more, no less) and that all deliveries are made on time as requested.

The suppliers have formal packaging policies, procedures and handling techniques in place that ensure all products are delivered in good condition, that all goods are free of any handling or in-transit damage. The suppliers are capable of meeting all current and future bar coding and labeling requirements and can ensure that all required documentation is supplied with the goods: all packing slips, invoices, certificates of compliance, test results, product data, prints, lot control data, freight bills, and any other requested documents.

**Order Entry Process Control.** Management monitors the suppliers' order entry processes with a goal of accurate and timely processing of all customer orders. This includes the entire process from the time an order is received to the time the invoice is paid. The performance measurements we will monitor include:

- the ease of placing an order.

- order entry accuracy.

- the order entry cycle time.

- pricing accuracy.

- picking accuracy.

- product quality.

- the completeness of each shipment.

- on-time deliveries.

- invoicing accuracy.

- resolution of customer complaints.

**Customer Service.** The suppliers are able to demonstrate that not only do they have a customer service function, but that it is clearly defined and supported by management. Senior management support is apparent by their review of the performance metrics to monitor customer service levels and the implementation of continuous improvement initiatives to aim for higher levels of customer service.

Response time is measured for all inquiries, whether they are for product information, for technical assistance or for general assistance. All lines of communication are available for customer assistance, as well as order entry, mail, phone, fax, EDI and the Web. The suppliers provide flexible delivery schedules and quantities without any negative effect on pricing. There is no extra charge for giving the customer what he wants or needs.

**Product Warranty and Reliability.** The suppliers have reliability built into their products and can demonstrate that this has been confirmed through DOE (Design of Experiments), FMEA (Failure Mode and Effects Analysis), or other similar analyses of their products in applications that are routinely experienced by their customers. They maintain documentation of the results and will provide them for review when requested.

Industry standard warranty periods are provided for all products and services the suppliers offer to their customers. A formal written procedure is in place for handling all warranty claims, and the suppliers can furnish documented evidence that they adhere to their procedure for processing them.

**Manufacturing Process Control.** The suppliers can demonstrate that their manufacturing processes are in control and predictable. They can show through the use of statistical process control or other methodologies that critical quality characteristics are measured and maintained. Any nonconformances are documented and corrective actions have been put in place. The suppliers routinely gather data from these analyses and uses them to initiate continuous improvement programs and further refine their manufacturing processes.

The suppliers are focused on building quality into the product instead of inspecting it in. The processes are properly documented and all production and installations are performed under controlled conditions. Prevention of defects being the motivating factor, only approved equipment and inspection techniques are used.

There are preventive maintenance programs in place as well as full calibration of all gages and tools. Tool tracking is also a part of process control. We all know that bad tools make bad parts. The suppliers should know the useful life of each of their tools and track the number of parts each tool has made. Suppliers that try to squeeze out a few extra parts are being penny wise and pound-foolish. If the tool life exceeds what was planned that is acceptable; using the tool beyond its life limits is not. Training programs for all employees are in place and directed at ensuring all employees are qualified for the work they are doing.

**Manufacturing Process Capability.** The suppliers can demonstrate that all of their internal processes are capable of meeting or exceeding the specifications and requirements of each customer's product or service. Statistical data and analysis are available, for all critical stations, to the customer.

**Management Commitment.** Though often talked about, this is an area that needs to be confirmed by deployment of customer's requirements in their vision statements and in their procedures. Management will have defined the level of expertise required for each job, and all personnel will be evaluated against those criteria before being allowed to perform those functions. Training records that demonstrate employee capabilities and skill levels will be available to customers for their review. Policies and procedures will be in place that will show how customer requirements are to be met. These will include many of the following:

- How customer orders will be processed and how they will be controlled throughout the manufacturing cycle

- How control will be established throughout all the direct and indirect functions of the company

- How employees will be trained and how they will be expected to maintain their skill levels

- If product or service defects are found, how they will be handled, including notification of the customer

- How the processes will be tested and then how the products will be tested

- Who in the organization is responsible for quality and how he/she will maintain his/her independence and objectivity

- How information will be processed and how it will be controlled

- Management's roles in assuring that all quality requirements are met

- Explicit, detailed instructions on how policies and procedures are to be implemented

- What is expected from each functional area

- Technical data, control parameters and specifications

**Quality Systems.** The suppliers have in place formal, well-documented quality systems that ensure continuous process control throughout all functions of the company (both direct and indirect). These are all processes that contribute to the manufacture and distribution of all products and services produced and delivered to customers: from receipt of materials to handling and storage, through the entire manufacturing process, to the distribution channels, and ending when the customer receivable is collected. The quality systems are based on statistical methodologies and comply with recognized quality standards for the markets they service.

Control and release of all nonconforming materials is clearly defined in the quality systems. The conditions that allow release and further processing of these materials is crystal-clear. The procedure will cover the isolation, identification, storage, and evaluation of all such materials. Items that cannot be reworked to meet customer specifications will be scrapped. The rework and/or scrap of this material will be in accordance with the guidelines approved by the customer. All nonconformances will be traced to the source and corrective measures put in place to prevent any further occurrences.

The quality system contains requirements for internal audits that will verify that all quality activities meet customer needs and specifications, as well as evaluate the effectiveness of the quality system. Management will periodically use this data to determine if any corrective action is required. Ingrained in the suppliers' quality systems will be the concept that "no measurement will ever be taken by an instrument of unknown accuracy." The quality systems will define the frequency of calibration, along with the selection, control, and maintenance of all test equipment.

**Quality Management.** The suppliers' organizational structures are designed to support and promote the quality focus that is required. There are formal written quality policies with measurable quality objectives and performance metrics. Lines of authority and quality responsibilities are clearly defined. Management supports "quality at the source." Training programs and operating policies promote operator control instead of the use of inspection methodologies.

Inspection techniques are used for incoming materials, in-process sampling, as well as at final stations. Inspectors are thoroughly trained, and all inspections are clearly defined, along with the responsible party and the frequency. Among the test procedures that are closely monitored by the supplier are:

- the equipment which will be used for the test.
- how and when samples will be taken.
- the method of recording the results.
- the results obtained versus the acceptance criteria.
- who the results are reported to.
- what actions are taken if the results fall outside of the acceptable limits.
- how the material is released for further processing.
- what corrective action is taken to correct the problem at the source.

**Research and Development.** Suppliers that have aggressive and innovative R&D departments are the kind of suppliers we want to include in our base. The number of patents they hold evidences the results of their R&D. These are the companies that will grow with us. They will be open to new ideas and new ways to cut costs. Since it is management philosophy that supports the investment in R&D, new ideas should permeate the supplier's business with continuous improvement projects.

**Compliance of Materials.** The suppliers' procurement processes ensure that all raw materials, finished goods, and subcontracted services meet or exceed the specifications of the customers' products and services. Compliance to specifications is confirmed through sampling, audits, supplier surveys, performance monitoring techniques and statistical methodologies. Where noncompliance is discovered, corrective actions are immediately put in place to prevent any further occurrences. The procurement systems are defined and procedures are in place that document how purchase orders are created, controlled, and authorized.

**Document Control Processes.** The suppliers maintain formal document control processes that cover bills of material, engineering change notices, process sheets, operation routings and drawing revision levels. The systems make these available to all appropriate operating personnel. The written procedures are incorporated into the suppliers' employee-training programs. Periodic audits are conducted to verify compliance with their procedures. Where required, customers are part of the engineering change process.

**Technical Support.** The suppliers use their expertise to provide technical support to their customers in order to improve current products, as well as during the design of new and future products and services. The support includes repair and installation services. Technically qualified sales engineers or technicians provide the technical support.

Problem resolution during the design and manufacture of new products is provided in an expeditious manner. This results in not only shorter design cycles with less rework and redesign, but also a smoother transition from design to manufacturing, and, overall, a shorter time to market, which should provide a competitive edge in the marketplace. These services should be provided at no cost or at a nominal cost to the customer.

**Financial Stability.** Suppliers are able to demonstrate that they are financially sound with stable management. A review of their financial statements (a 10K would be advisable) should reveal whether or not they use their assets effectively to generate cash flows from internal operations that are sufficient to sustain continued business operations. Suppliers that are willing to share this information demonstrate openness and a willingness to enter into a long-term relationship based on trust. The suppliers should also agree that any changes in their financial condition, ownership of the company, or their senior management will be shared with their customers immediately.

**Cost Controls.** Cost containment is a key objective for the suppliers, as it makes good business sense. Suppliers are actively involved in cost reduction programs. They are able to show the gains made by previous programs and demonstrate how they were able to reduce product and service costs. The suppliers are willing to share these savings with their customers. They work closely with their customers in setting cost reduction goals, as well as embarking on joint projects that are mutually beneficial.

**Business and Industry Knowledge.** All of the suppliers' employees and all of their representatives are knowledgeable about the industry they represent. The suppliers are leaders in their fields, as evidenced by their involvement and active participation in trade groups and technical associations. Their expertise is sought after by industry publications to which they will be regular contributors. It provides insight into the trends that are taking place in its industry, and it utilizes this information in assisting its customers in preparing for the next generation of products.

**Facilities Management.** The suppliers' facilities and equipment are clean and well maintained, such that they pose no threat to the continuous, uninterrupted flow of quality products and services to the customers. Housekeeping is a major part of good facilities management. I have seen plants where the floors are so clean you can eat off them. I have also seen the results of cleaning up dirty plants, ones where machine operators can now come to work in white shirts. They enjoy the new working environment so much that they each take part in keeping it that way. Utilizing programs of preventive or predictive maintenance the supplier will be able to keep downtime to an absolute minimum. Analysis, such as MTBF (Mean Time Between Failures), is used to create the maintenance programs which are scheduled for off-hours. The operators, however, should do routine servicing, while machines are running. In addition, facilities management contains provisions for safety-related monitoring to ensure that a safe work place is provided.

**Compliance to Regulations.** The suppliers are able to demonstrate that they are in compliance with all applicable government regulations. These include all federal, state and local requirements, including those associated with:

- OSHA, the Occupational Safety and Health Administration.

- EEOC, the Equal Employment Opportunity Commission.

- EPA, the Environmental Protection Agency.

- all regulations dealing with the handling and disposing of hazardous waste.

Compliance to all regulations will not be limited to the manufacturing processes. All products that contain chemicals covered by the regulations are properly labeled. In addition, suppliers are good neighbors and citizens, taking part in the protection and well being of the communities in which they operate.

**Ethics.** Companies must operate in an ethical manner, and their compliance is their choice of an operating philosophy.

**Labor Relations.** Recognizing that their most important asset is their people, the suppliers have in place programs that promote excellent working conditions and a stable, highly productive work force. Whether the shops are union or nonunion, experience has shown that employees who are treated with respect and listened to build quality parts. The suppliers are equal opportunity employers and have safety programs in place that ensure safe working environments for all their employees.

Employee involvement, employee empowerment and self-directed work are evident or in the process of being implemented. Training programs that are geared toward enhancing employee skills, as well as providing educational opportunities, are also apparent. The suppliers are able to demonstrate that their labor relations are sound and pose no threat to delivery schedules or quality levels for all products and services provided to the customer.

**Logistics.** The suppliers' plants are located near requisite transportation facilities (airports, docks, railroads, even major roadways). This ensures that the suppliers will not only have a access to a steady stream of quality materials to supply their operations, but will also be able to deliver their products and services to their customers economically and in a timely manner.

Additionally, we need to consider the effect on our limited resources if our suppliers are in remote, hard to reach locations. Our rule should be to first look at suppliers who are within 60 minutes of our plant. Otherwise, our ability to visit more than one supplier in a day becomes more limited. If for any reason it becomes necessary to send a team in to a distant supplier site, it becomes very expensive. Freight costs will also increase.

## STRATEGIC PARTNER METHODOLOGY

## CHAPTER SIX

## Definition

Webster defines partner as: "One who shares; one of two or more persons who play together against an opposing side; one of the heavy timbers that strengthen a ship's deck to support a mast." All of these definitions can be used to describe the relationships we need to develop with those suppliers that we have deemed critical to our success in the marketplace.

In our cases we will be developing a partnering relationship with more than one supplier. The results we obtained from our use of the Material Positioning Grid will more than likely point to a number of commodities or items that are mission critical. The suppliers that provide us with those materials are the ones that we need to develop those extraordinarily close relationships that we both can use to grow into the next generation of products. And by the way, if there is currently no supplier that meets our needs for this alliance, then we need to be nurturing and developing a new one. This means taking a supplier of similar products and growing them into the kind of supplier we will need to continue our success.

## Benefits of Partnership

It should not be necessary at this point to explicitly detail the benefits of partnering. What follows is a brief review.

**Easier Sourcing.** If we have already recognized a supplier that is the most efficient producer with the best quality and the lowest costs, why would we look anywhere else?

**Long-term Relationship.** A long-term relationship eliminates the costs associated with finding and cultivating new sources. The time and energy that would have been spent can now be more profitably utilized.

**Win/Win Relationship.** This is actually a win/win/win relationship, because not only do we both share in cost savings, but our customers will also. Additionally we both share in new business as we gain market share.

**Single-Sourcing.** It should no be longer necessary to split our requirements with multiple sources. Having a supplier that can deliver 100% of our requirements, 100% on time, with 100% quality, 100% of the time, is really all we need, which in addition to the savings of working with a single supplier also brings us the benefits of being able to leverage larger volumes.

**Trust, Loyalty, Honesty and Integrity.** These are the cornerstones of this alliance. It makes for free and easier communication, as well as an enhanced working relationship at all levels of both organizations. This is true for both sides.

**Design Capability.** We expect the producers of our mission critical materials to be at the leading/emerging edge of technology. They, therefore, have design capability that we can capitalize on, not only in the development of future products, but also in the best way to incorporate their materials into our current products.

**ESI (Early Supplier Involvement).** Having this close relationship coupled with the fact that we are looking for single-sourcing allows us to have our suppliers involved at the earliest stages of product design. As we know from being in the reverse position (getting our suppliers involved too late) this will result in a better product. It will also eliminate much of the redesign that results from finding out too late that we overestimated or underestimated the capabilities of a supplier or product.

**Mutually Acceptable Specifications.** Working so closely with our suppliers and having them involved early in the process means that we will have agreed upon specifications at ever point in the process.

**Improved Profitability.** Eliminating the costs of multiple sources, utilizing the most efficient suppliers, eliminating the costs associated with poor quality, eliminating the costs of carrying inventory, shortening the design process and being first to market with the best product all translate into improved profitability.

**Confidentiality of Information Shared.** This is critical. Being able to share proprietary information with suppliers (both theirs and ours) without worrying about the consequences of it being misused means we can get the early supplier involvement that means so much to our continued success.

**Technical Support.** We can expect technical support from our partners at all phases and levels of the process, from the design of the product through the manufacture of the product to support in the field. This includes assistance with any marketing efforts that require technical knowledge as well as any failure analysis that is required.

**Reliable Performance.** We should be seeing reduced cycle times, receiving excellent quality, getting as-required deliveries, and buying at the least total cost.

**Supplier Improvement Programs.** These should always be in place and are ongoing. Initiated by our suppliers, these programs are aimed not only at cost reduction but also at improved quality and technologically advanced designs.

## Characteristics of a Partner Candidate

What kind of suppliers are we looking for? Remember we are developing a long-term relationship. These are suppliers that are not only critical to our success in today's marketplace; these are suppliers that we are going to incorporate into the plans for our future. As we discussed in Chapter Three, suppliers should meet certain minimum characteristics that make them the kind of supplier we would want to partner with. These criteria include:

- financial stability.
- organizational stability.
- quality management.
- quality system deployment.
- good customer service.
- emerging technology.
- interest in our success.
- technical support.
- cost reduction goals.
- self-measuring.
- being an efficient producer.
- shorter lead times.
- willingness to partner.

## Stages of the Partnering Methodology

There are four basic stages to the partnering methodology. They are:

I   **Background and Documentation.** This stage is

the gathering of all the information necessary to create and sustain this long-term relationship.

II  **Process Evaluation.** This stage makes sure we know, understand and rate highly everything there is to know about the way our intended partner produces product, as well as how it runs its company.

III  **Detail Formulation.** This stage acknowledges that any corrective action has taken place and encompasses laying out and negotiating all the details of how the partnership will operate.

IV  **Audit and Maintenance and Commitment**. This ongoing stage reviews the results of the relationship, takes any corrective action required, and plans for the future, incorporating strategic changes to the partnership.

Let's examine each of these stages a little more closely.

## Stage I - Background and Documentation

This stage gathers together much of the information we already have, as well as additional information that can easily be requested from the supplier. Again we must always remember that suppliers touch more than one area of the company. Almost every functional area has information, direct or indirect, about our suppliers, which is all the more reason for using cross-functional teams wherever we can.

**Internal Sources**

• **IT.** Our own company database contains important information relative to delivery status, purchasing status, quality history, cost status, etc. We may even have some measurements in place. We should be able to get the following minimum data, encompassing performance and quality statistics and history.

- The number of lots delivered on time vs. the total number of lots delivered

- The number of purchase orders on time vs. the total number of purchase orders

- Dollarized versions of the above two measurements

- The number of lots accepted vs. the total number of lots received

- The number of defects per lot

- The types of defects

- The number of purchase orders we place with this supplier a year

- The number of dollars we spend with this supplier

- The number of different things we buy from this supplier

- **Service.** Our service department deals with the performance of our products in the field. Since we are looking at mission critical components and materials, any field failures would certainly have information as to exactly what failed and, hopefully, why. Additionally from this department we get maintenance information that should detail the number of times we routinely replace these components even before there has been a field failure, and, of course, the type of support we received from the supplier whenever these situations arose.

- **Engineering.** Our engineering department has additional information for us.

  - How involved and supportive was the supplier during the initial design phases?

  - What is the quality of its documentation, especially as it relates to our specifications?

  - What were the Engineering reasons for its original selection as a supplier?

- **Quality.** Our quality department should be able to provide additional information about the supplier's quality performance. Since it is Quality that usually heads up the Material Review Board, we should be able to get its analysis of any defects found, as well as the results of any corrective action that was taken. This information should also include the supplier's attitude and willingness to make any changes necessary to improve its quality.

  Quality should have a great deal of information gathered from on-site quality surveys. It should have knowledge of the supplier's quality system and quality commitment along with an assessment of the suppler's manufacturing capabilities.

- **Finance.** Making sure our finance department is always included on our cross-functional teams and involved in as much of the process as we can, should yield three important types of information for us.

- **Financial Stability.** Review Dun and Bradstreet type ratings, ownership information and financial relationships (ratios) that measure the health of an organization.

- **Cost information.** This includes all factors that affect the pricing of the things we purchase from this supplier.

- **An analysis of the structure of the supplier's company and departments which may be operating inefficiently.** Remember, we are looking for the most efficient providers who keep total costs down so that our costs do not include excessive overhead.

### External Information From Our Supplier

Our supplier should be able to provide the following kinds of information from its records.

- **Performance.** Measurements of its own performance; its delivery performance, total cycle time performance, as well as its quality performance

- **Its Internal Systems.** Copies of its own manuals and supporting documentation for the way it runs its business

- **Quality.** Quality manuals, quality policies, along with supporting documentation of its adherence to its own policies

- **Preventive Maintenance.** How it keeps its machines and processes at optimal performance and reduces interruptions caused by machine failure

- **Tooling and Gages.** What system is in place? How does it work?

- **Survey Results.** The results of any pre-survey or self-evaluation to our quality standards that we may have sent

## Documentation Stage Status Report

All of this information that we have managed to gather should be condensed down into a readable, manageable document that the team can digest. The Document Stage Status Report should be in a consistent format so that subsequent reports are all consumed and evaluated the same way.

## Stage II - Process Evaluation

During this stage, we have two important objectives that need to be accomplished.

- To evaluate and effectively measure the supplier's processes

- To spell out any corrective action required before we will take the next step of becoming partners

Evaluating the supplier's processes is akin to a formal quality survey. As such, it will take a great deal of planning. We will want to make sure that we have accounted for all of the following:

- Selecting the right members for the team

- Assessing the skill levels required for success and providing training to ensure all of the required skill levels are present on the team

- Allowing enough time at the supplier's site to accomplish our objectives

- Creating a detailed schedule of what we expect to see in each functional area of the company and with whom we need to meet

- Coordinating this with our supplier so it has everything and everyone in place for us

- Deciding on the objective criteria that we will measure the supplier with (Once we agree on how an area is to be rated there should be no arguments.)

- Allowing time for some private meetings for us to review our progress against our formal agenda (If we are not sure of whether we saw what we needed to see, we can then ask for further documentation.)

The second objective involves the compilation of our findings and meeting with the supplier to discuss corrective action he believes is necessary. It is important to note that we expect the supplier to agree with our findings, recognize that corrective action is required and put a detailed action plan in place, plan with key milestones and measurements.

## Stage III – Detail Formulation

During this stage, we are going to first make sure that any corrective action that was required did take place. Assuming that all is as we both expect it to be, we can hammer out and formalize the details of the partnership.

It is always important to reduce these agreements to writing. Like any other partnership, circumstances change over time. These days, with mergers and acquisitions at an all time high, people change, markets change, economies change and ownership changes. If there is either no longer a reason to continue the partnership or the partnership is not working out, there should be an agreement in place as to how it is to dissolve.

The agreement should include but not be limited to:

- purpose and scope of the partnership.
- duration of the agreement.
- clearly detailed responsibilities of each of the parties.
- implementation of engineering changes, including the methodology and the sharing of any costs involved.
- quality expected (We already know it is zero defects.) and agreed upon. This should also include any additional documentation required, such as those related to the measurement of internal processes and the analysis of internal failures.

- inspection requirements: what, by whom and when. (Remember: quality at the source.)

- delivery commitments.

- warranties expected.

- pricing formulas for existing products (not tied to inflation). Agreement on exactly what will cause the price to increase or decrease and on pricing formulas for new products.

- payment terms and conditions.

- cost reduction targets.

- forecasting, scheduling and order processing details.

- lead times expected, as well as any capacity limitations.

- first article qualifications when required.

- end of life planning.

- formal review meetings to evaluate quality, performance, product design, product enhancements and product direction.

- communication methodology, designation of company liaisons and expected reports.

- confidentiality concerning all proprietary products, processes, marketing plans and product direction on both sides .

- exclusivity of access to covered products.

- Force Majeure – Let us not forget Mother Nature,

the power of unions and any other natural or un-natural disaster that can occur.

- limits of liabilities as appropriate.
- termination clauses.

### Stage IV – Audit and Maintenance and Commitment

During this stage we are going to make sure that we are receiving what we have agreed upon. This merely means putting some measurements in place that will act as early warning signals if any part of the agreement begin to show signs of deteriorating.

## Two-Way Street

Just a reminder that a partnership is a two-way street. We also need to put in place those measurements that will assure us that we are meeting our part of any agreement. A partnership like anything else takes commitment, effort, nurturing and a sincere desire to make sure it succeeds.

# TYPICAL SUPPLIER STRATEGIES

# CHAPTER SEVEN

## Appropriate Strategies

Having determined where on the Material Positioning Matrix our commodity has fallen, we want to begin the process of selecting an appropriate strategy or strategies. As we discussed in the previous chapter there is no single strategy that works every time. There are, however, a number of typical strategies that have shown themselves to be effective in each of the various quadrants of the matrix. It is up to us to determine which one(s) actually fit the current situation.

Our selection will be dependent on the strength of the indices, the location of the position on the matrix, and our own knowledge of the commodity, the industry and our supplier base. We need to evaluate each of the strategies and select the one(s) we feel will have the best chance of success.

We may actually select more than one strategy where we believe it is fitting. It is also possible that we may decide to use a strategy that normally works best in a different quadrant. Bear in mind that where we are with our current sourcing methodology may influence our choices.

Figure 7.1 is a strategy matrix that shows where the typical strategies have been found to be effective. Let's examine the typical strategies a little more closely:

**Partner/Alliance**. This strategy is used for mission critical material. As we discussed in great detail in Chapter Six, this is a long and expensive process. It is not really worth the time or the expense if other less costly strategies will achieve the same results.

This is a long-term relationship we are seeking. It will involve early supplier involvement in the design of our products. We will expect this supplier to be on the leading edge of the design of its products. In fact we expect that the supplier will be working with us to look at the future of our products, and that it will be designing with us in mind. We will be looking for continuous improvement programs in all of the functional areas of this supplier as we look to reduce cost as well as cycle time.

## STRATEGY MATRIX

| | STRATEGIC | LEVERAGE | BOTTLENECK | NONCRITICAL |
|---|:---:|:---:|:---:|:---:|
| Partner/Alliance | X | | | |
| Cultivating Suppliers | X | X | X | |
| Long-Term Agreement/Contract | X | X | X | X |
| Standardize | X | X | X | X |
| Quality Improvement | X | X | | |
| Overhead Cost Reduction | X | X | | X |
| Consolidate With Other Divisions | | X | | X |
| Competitive Bidding | | X | | X |
| Price Rollback | | X | | X |
| Supplier Reduction | | X | | X |
| Cross Commodity Leveraging | | X | X | X |
| Internal Price Benchmarking | | X | X | X |
| Re-source to New Suppliers | | | X | |
| Substitute | | | X | |

Figure 7.1

We have observed a shift in the marketplace where companies are looking for commodity managers with buyers or buyer/planners working for them. The expectation is that the commodity managers will really understand their commodity, its history, its current trend in the marketplace and where the industry is headed. Where a particular commodity becomes mission critical, having a commodity manager could be a make or break situation.

Take the case of a Chicago-based telecommunications company. Its products have become dependent on chip technology and, possibly even more important, chip availability. It also has a very short product life cycle. As technology advances, its products become outdated within six months. If it does not have the next generation ready for the marketplace, it begins to lose market share. It was essential that this company align itself with a chip provider, partially to influence the design of new chips, making sure that the supplier knew where its products were headed, and partially to ensure that it had priority in the allocation of product when supplies were scarce.

Another case comes to mind that illustrates the additional benefits of working this closely with a supplier. A California computer company plant had just such a relationship with a plastics house that supplied parts for the its computers. As was customary, production people from suppliers would periodically visit the plant to see how their products were used in the production process. On one such visit the injection molder that made the base plate was watching it being fabricated into the next higher assembly. The first operation was to insert the feet into the base plate.

As he watched he saw an opportunity. In the process of injection molding, dry plastic pellets are melted and injected into cavity molds under pressure and allowed to cool and harden. The larger the piece being molded the longer the process takes. For larger parts, the supplier can often only make one or two pieces at a time. During that time the operator has virtually nothing to do, even if he is running more than one molding machine at a time. He is really an observer ensuring the machines have not malfunctioned and have a sufficient supply of plastic pellets.

He suggested that he could perform this operation for the computer company during the time that he was not really busy. Consequently, since the cost of the operator was already in the base plate that they were supplying, the plastics company could perform this operation at little added cost. This is truly a *win-win* situation. The plastics company would make some additional profit, and the computer company would actually have both a cost and a cycle time reduction.

**Cultivating Suppliers.** Every now and again we have to grow our own suppliers. We need to start with a good foundation. Selecting a supplier from our preferred supplier list is a good first step. If we can find a supplier where our new items would be the next logical step for the supplier, even better. If not, how easy would it be for the supplier to acquire and/or develop the necessary skills and equipment? We have a role to play here. We are going to grow this capability, which means we may have to lay out some capital, may have to provide some technical expertise, may have to do some training, and may have to baby-sit the development process. Helping our preferred suppliers is our contribution to the relationship.

**Long-term Agreement/Contract.** Negotiate long-term agreements with some very specific goals in mind: reducing or stabilizing our pricing over the long run so there are no unexpected surprises that will give us grief later on, locking in an allocation to ensure a steady stream of needed materials and make sure that we can produce enough product to meet our demand, and agreeing on deliveries that support the way we intend to build product. Longer-term agreements can be used to detail expected redesign efforts that will provide cost reductions or quality improvements in the future. Suppliers are more willing to agree to these changes if they know they will have enough business in the future to warrant the investment. In this way we also move them closer to sharing in the required investment instead of us having to fund it in its *entirety*.

**Standardize.** Standardize! Standardize! Standardize! I just cannot say that enough times. I have worked with so many companies that never really understood the benefits of standardization. Or, if they did understand, they were unwilling or unable to control it. Standardization ought to be a management policy, and we should have every engineer's performance and salary reviews tied to how well he/she standardizes.

Nonstandard parts cost more. It doesn't get any simpler than that. Nonstandard parts cost more to design and cost more to buy. We generally have to wait longer for the parts and have to plan farther ahead. How much better off would we be if we redesigned the product to use an industry standard design? Or we may want to redesign in order to eliminate product proliferation.

Have we not seen the same items in our item master with more than one item number? I can remember one company I worked with that had three different item numbers for red paint. Do we need every size screw that was ever designed? Or can we standardize and skip a few sizes in order to reduce the number of items we have to purchase, store and issue? Do we need to have every type of head for each of the screws (pan head, phillips head, slotted head, and flat head)? Do we also need to have screws made out of multiple materials (brass, stainless steel, titanium, and other alloys)? Do we need them to be plated, anodized, galvanized, and hardened? The fewer variations we have, the easier it is to control them. We can buy them in larger quantities, with fewer POs, handling them fewer times, and will use less space in our stock-rooms. They will be easier to plan for and less costly in the long run. Every engineer should be trained to look at what we own before designing in a new variation when what we have will do nicely.

**Quality Improvement.** This entails working with our suppliers to help them improve the quality of their products, instead of just going elsewhere. We should approach their quality the same way we would do our own manufacturing facility. An important step in this process is to integrate our suppliers' people into the improvement team. It is absolutely essential that they buy into the process, and agree with the changes that need to be made. Knowledge transfer has to take place to ensure that they are able to sustain the improvements once we leave.

First on the list is a process mapping to see how the process actually works, *not* how we think it works. We would also do a capability study to determine exactly what the process is capable of producing. Taking the *as-is* process into account we can lay out the *to-be* process. Once the changes are made, we need to implement process control to ensure that the process remains in control. With process control, we can institute corrective measures when a process begins to go out of control before we allow the process to produce bad parts. A process that is in control will consistently produce parts to specifications that are within its capability.

**Overhead Cost Reduction.** It is always important to remember that a portion of the price we pay is to cover the cost of overhead. And in many cases this far exceeds the raw cost of the product itself. I therefore feel very justified in reviewing those costs with my preferred suppliers. When we look at the whole picture with this frame of mind, we can begin to see other fertile areas for cost-related improvements that should show themselves by reducing the price we pay for materials. Overhead includes the cost of R&D, Finance, Design Engineering, Quality Assurance, Manufacturing, Engineering, Human Resources, Materials Management (which includes Planning, Purchasing, Production Control, Inventory Management, Shipping and Receiving), Marketing, Sales, Information Technology, Order Entry, and Manufacturing Operations. Cost reductions in some of these areas not only reduce my supplier's overhead and make him a more efficient producer, but should also show up in our costs and in cycle time reductions.

I mentioned before the California computer company's plant. When this plant was set up it was set up as a single product plant. The suppliers were hand picked and agreed to operate in a Just-in-Time mode. All of the selected suppliers were local and capable of daily deliveries. Production schedules were sent to all of the suppliers with the daily production rates. The rates were kept constant in the short term. The suppliers delivered daily quantities of defect-free materials directly to the production line in nested containers. If a quality problem arose or a quantity of parts was shorted, the suppliers remedied the situation immediately.

At the end of the month, the computer company took the number of computers shipped, multiplied it times the Bill of Material and sent the suppliers a check or electronically deposited the funds in the suppliers' accounts. The theory was that if they made and shipped the computers, they must have had all of the parts required. Look at the tremendous advantages and cost savings for both sides.

### Computer Company's Benefits:

- No Purchase Orders or Blanket Releases made or issued, which also means no PO files in Purchasing, Receiving, Quality or Accounts Payable

- No inspection or inspection reports for incoming parts

- No receiving or receiving reports

- No handling of inventory into and out of the stockroom (no unpacking, picking or repackaging)
- No stockroom to speak of
- No matching of receiving reports to POs; no filing of receiving reports
- No invoices to be processed
- Minimal freight costs (all local deliveries using company trucks)

**Supplier's Benefits:**
- No POs to file
- No Order Entry required for these parts
- No invoices to prepare
- No receivables beyond the month
- A stable schedule to plan against
- No shipping documents
- Reduced packaging costs, reusable KanBan containers
- Visibility

**Consolidate With Other Divisions.** Use the buying power of the entire corporation to negotiate better prices, deliveries, terms and conditions. Often times we find that in giving business units and divisions autonomy to control their own destiny, we lose some of the cooperation that we should be seeing between them. If we do not already have a corporate purchasing council, we need to put one together, made up of representatives of each of the business units.

The council's charter is to gather information from each of the divisions to understand just how much the corporation is spending on each of the commodities used. A commodity team made up of members from the divisions that use that commodity the most should be mapping out a procurement strategy that addresses the needs of the corporation as a whole and also leverages the buying power of the corporation. This team should then select and negotiate with suppliers that can meet the corporation's needs.

There are some other key things the council could be working on, such as the standardization of the procurement process, forms, terms and conditions, as well as software and systems, and lastly putting together a training program that can be used by all of the divisions to enhance the skills of the purchasing departments, educate them as to the latest methodologies and ideas, and provide a forum to share ideas. The forum would utilize the purchasing knowledge within the corporation to solve problems in the divisions when they occur or, even anticipate them and proactively prevent their occurrence.

**Competitive Bidding.** Most procurements in the beginning should be competitively bid. This gives two or more suppliers an opportunity to show us just how much they want our business. Be careful here. Remember we are looking at *least total cost* over the long term. An initial low price is not the criteria that will sustain an ongoing relationship. We should be laying out the criteria that the successful supplier will have to meet. Competitive bidding works quite well when there are multiple suppliers that can meet our needs. (This means all of our needs, including delivery, quality, price, selection, service, design and technical assistance, etc.)

We will probably use competitive bidding for many of our noncritical parts where we will be looking for a single supplier to handle as many of them as possible. It is a strategy that also works well for leveraged components. In the future, as we whittle down the supplier base, we will be looking at single-sourcing many of our procurements. As we get closer to partnering relationships, and continue to assist our suppliers in becoming the most efficient producers, competitive procurement becomes a waste of time. We are even beginning to see the Department of Defense (DOD) back away from requiring competitive bids in many cases. Initially only willing to do this in emergency situations, the DOD is now waiving the requirement when we can demonstrate that the rationale does not go against the intent of the requirement. This is only a *ray of hope*. Congress still has numerous laws on the books (over 800 last time I checked) governing the procurement process the government has to follow that will have to be changed.

The selected supplier will be one where we have a close enough relationship that we are in full agreement with its cost structure and profit margins and where we consistently select that supplier as the most efficient supplier and, therefore, the one with the lowest total cost.

**Price Rollback.** When we get responses to our RFQs, we may find bids that are lower than some of our preferred suppliers. In addition, as other suppliers look to gain a share of our business they may submit unsolicited bids for commodities that they know we use on a regular basis. We can use these quotes to ask our suppliers to roll back their prices to meet those of other suppliers. You never know how much is still on the table until you ask. It is also a certainty that you will not get what you do not ask for. A word of caution here, we want our suppliers to be profitable. As I've mentioned before, if our business is not profitable for the supplier, we will not get the results we need.

If a supplier cannot meet the other quotes, it may be a sign of inefficiencies in its organization, which means it either becomes a candidate for some continuous improvement activities or a candidate for replacement.

**Supplier Reduction.** Chapter Two was devoted to reducing the supplier base, so it is not necessary to reiterate all of the benefits here. The fewer the number of suppliers that we have to deal with, the more manageable the entire procurement process becomes. Every step of the process will be done fewer times, which lowers our cost of doing business. At the same time it increases our leverage as the remaining suppliers will have a larger share of our procurement dollars.

**Cross Commodity Leverage.** Sourcing with suppliers that handle multiple commodities allows us to leverage our buying power by placing more of our dollars with a single supplier. While we sometimes certify a supplier for a single item only, in this case we are looking for suppliers that are equally as good with more than one commodity.

**Internal Price Benchmarking.** Let's not forget our own plants when sourcing. Usually our make/buy policies are dictated and, therefore, the calculations we use to determine pricing are weighted to support the policy. Running through the numbers, the decision always comes out the same. We either make everything in-house or we out-source everything. Buyers and engineers figure this out pretty quickly, and the decisions go on being made the same way, whether or not they make good business sense.

I have always allowed our own plant to bid on items along with our outside suppliers. Our buyers and engineers know that the criteria we will use for the cost part of the selection will be least total cost. By the way, if they successfully bid in-house and then do not meet their cost estimates, they need some pretty solid rationale to explain what happened. Keeping items in-house for sound business reasons, such as a proprietary product or process or stabilizing the work force, always takes precedence.

We can use our internal capabilities to determine what an item should cost. We then have some ammunition when we sit down at the bargaining table. Knowing the cost of the raw materials, any dedicated or tailored capital equipment required, labor costs and approximate overhead can give us an edge during negotiations. Always keep in mind that we are not trying to beat our suppliers into submission. We want them to make a reasonable profit, that is the only way they can stay in business. Remember our part of any bargain is to be a good customer. If we take all of the profit away from our suppliers, they will have no incentive to perform. They will only work on our products when they have nothing else to do. The results will be poor delivery performance and equally poor quality.

**Re-source To New Suppliers.** This is a relatively simple strategy. If a supplier is not fulfilling our needs and is not willing to accept our assistance in improving its processes (manufacturing or otherwise), the supplier needs to be replaced. We tend to hang onto suppliers far longer than we should. Whether this is because of personal feelings, a lack of time to address the problem, an unwillingness to admit we made a mistake, a lack of initiative, a lack of objective data or just plain procrastination does not matter. Suppliers that are not striving to be better do not really deserve our consideration. Unfortunately they also consume an inordinate amount of our time as we try to remedy the problems they cause us.

An aerospace and defense company I worked with purchased titanium gears that needed to be nitrided. The supplier never delivered the gears to specification. The nitriding process, a type of hardening process, distorted the dimensions, and the distortion was not consistent in either direction. Two years and hundreds of thousands of dollars later, the aerospace company threw in the towel and went looking for a new supplier.

The initial selection was obviously not thorough. The original supplier was not capable of producing gears to the specifications. (We would later find out that no one could.) The supplier's process was not capable of meeting the industry standards. The supplier had inspection equipment that could inspect to the industry standard, but its employees did not know how to use it. The supplier subcontracted the nitriding process to a supplier that did not have a certified process. Additionally the original supplier did not understand its own process capability.

The first thing the new supplier did, before he would quote, was ask for changes to the prints and specifications. What had been asked for was impossible. After the changes were made, the new supplier delivered the gears, accurate to the new prints and specifications, in a relatively short time.

I should point out that this strategy is not contradictory to the philosophies I have espoused throughout. We do have an obligation to help our suppliers be successful. And we should do everything within reason to accomplish this. However, if a mistake has been made, and an inappropriate supplier chosen, the sooner we remedy the situation the better off we will be.

**Substitute.** When the material or component winds up in the bottleneck quadrant we should think about its replacement. A pure bottleneck component has a good deal of procurement risk. Yet, it also has a minimal, if any, effect on our success in the marketplace. In other words, this item is more trouble than it is worth. It is time to find a substitute material or component that is easier to procure. In the absence of a viable substitute, a redesign is called for. Let's face it, an item that has considerable procurement risk will consume a disproportionate share of a very scarce resource: our buyers' time. And why run the risk of not having enough material to make our shipments? Are we masochistic? Do we need this headache? After all, if the material is not here and production stops, it is always our fault. We want our buyers to concentrate on those items that are mission critical and not spend their time and concentration on the less significant.

# GLOBAL STRATEGIES

## CHAPTER EIGHT

It is not really possible to do much more than give you a flavor for global strategies in a single chapter. Entire books have been written on the subject. A good source for further information is Lee Krotseng's *Global Sourcing* (PT Publications; West Palm Beach, FL). Here we will touch briefly on a number of key areas.

- Reasons for going offshore
- Understanding the country climate
- Making contact
- Customs and linguistic differences
- Logistics and time considerations

---

• Managing remote suppliers
• Legal and social considerations

## Why Go Offshore?

The primary reason for looking at offshore sources has been and continues to be cost. Products that have a high labor content will definitely benefit from those countries that have relatively cheap labor. In recent years we have found a number of other reasons to go offshore. Technology being developed in other countries, although originally copied from the United States, is in some cases superior to what is available here. Those countries that support their economies by subsidizing their industrial growth are able to produce high-tech products (that do not have high labor content) at competitive prices, even when we take into account the cost of transporting these products into our country. Countries that have worked their manufacturing capabilities and processes along the continuous improvement continuum are able to produce products of higher quality, more consistently than we can. And, they can deliver at lower prices.

Think for a minute about Japan and the steel industry. Japan has no natural resources. The raw materials it needs to produce steel must be imported. Despite these obstacles, the country was able to produce steel, ship it across the ocean and sell it to us for less than it cost us to produce our own. As a result, many steel mills in our country have shut down their operations. They learned too late about the necessity of streamlining their operations and becoming more efficient producers.

A large U.S. office machine manufacturer did not become serious about quality and continuous improvement until it bought a Japanese competitor's copier. The U.S. company purchased the copier at a retail price which was less than it cost them to produce a similar copier. Of course, the company didn't believe it, so it went though the numbers at least two more times. The numbers were right. It was then that the U.S. manufacturer realized it had to change. If it did not become more efficient, it would soon be out of business.

What happened to television manufacturing in the U.S.? First the Japanese copied our designs, and then they worked on their ability to improve on the design of products. At one Japanese electronics company there is no final test for its television sets. The quality of the assemblies that go into the sets is so good that workers put the sets together and pack them right into boxes. The televisions work the first time, every time, right out of the box. In this industry and others, the Japanese have forced the world into higher levels of quality and customer service.

Buying offshore can provide us with lower cost items, higher quality items, and in some cases, more technologically advanced products. As countries like Japan move toward higher technology, there are other emerging countries ready to supply the cheaper labor and the products which are produced by that cheap labor. There are also many things that cannot be produced in this country because we have laws preventing the use of the chemicals and/or materials that go into them. I worked with a manufacturer of radomes (the front end of the plane that the radar looks through) for military aircraft. They added a layer of foam in the center to reduce the weight of the radome and at the same time not interfere with the radar signals. The foam was produced in just one European country. The foam could not be manufactured in the U.S. because the government considered one of the chemical ingredients hazardous.

With the war machine in this country winding down, we are now selling military planes, helicopters, weapons systems and other products to foreign governments. In order to help balance trade deficits, many of these foreign governments are requiring the products we sell to them have some percentage of local content. Often we are able to fulfill this obligation by spending some amount of dollars on products made there. In some countries reciprocity between privately-owned companies is illegal, and in some it is a common form of business.

## The Country Climate

How do we decide which countries we are willing to do business in? It is important to understand the country's climate, before we even begin to look for a new supplier (and I don't mean the weather either). The environment in which we will have to operate presents the amount of risk we will have to take. This in turn will affect the profitability of the procurement. In their book *Global Purchasing* Thomas and William Hickman point out that those countries that consistently have the best performance as exporters share three main characteristics:

- little/no political volatility.

- a firmly established internal framework of transportation, communication and financial systems.

- relatively large pool of knowledgeable personnel from non-rural areas.

**Political Volatility.** A politically volatile environment is literally a crapshoot. You have no idea what may happen or when. As the various factions take positions of leadership, the policies of the country are likely to change. One government may be pro-trade and one anti-trade. Sanctions, tariffs and other trade restrictions rear their ugly heads outside the country as the rest of the world tries to influence the course of development and political ideology. Other times trade restrictions may come from inside the country when its government has little interest in participating in a global economy.

But more important is the fact that politically volatile countries do not grow and develop in a way that encourages foreign investment or trade. Their economies remain poor and strained as dollars go into strengthening the military as a way of retaining control. They are unable to provide the internal framework that is so necessary if exporting is going to survive. It will be important for us to monitor conditions in whatever country we select, in order to give ourselves time to react to changing political trends. The Hickmans point out that political consistency is more important than the form of government.

**Sound Internal Framework.** The internal framework provides all of the things necessary to support foreign trade, as well as local economic development.

Since one of the things we need from any source is dependability, it is vital that the existing conditions do not undermine our suppliers' ability to keep their promises. No matter how well intentioned suppliers are, the lack of the necessary framework can easily prevent them from meeting their commitments.

A good transportation system, including roads, filling stations, repair facilities, and terminals, is necessary to bring raw materials to the producing plant as well as getting the products from the plant to the ports and then out of the country. The transportation system is also required to bring people to and from the workplace. Automobile ownership is not as widespread as it is in the United States.

A dependable communications system is the next important part of the internal framework. Clear communication between us and the producing plant is vital. Think of all the things that require communication during the procurement process. To begin with, we have RFIs, RFQs, negotiating terms and conditions, placing orders, confirming orders, making changes, and monitoring deliveries, not to mention confirming credit, expediting, and resolving problems.

In addition to language differences affecting communications, we may also need to consider the logistics of making a simple phone call. In many parts of the world, telephones are few and far between. Calls need to be booked ahead of time, and the quality of the lines is not good.

The last part of the internal framework is banking and financial services. The producing plant needs to pay its suppliers for goods and services in a timely manner. In countries with weak currencies and poor financial services, suppliers will not always deliver without funds up front. This can slow the process down adding to the product lead time.

**Personnel.** In order for the producing plants to sustain their operations a relatively large pool of knowledgeable personnel from non-rural areas is required. Where the transportation system is undeveloped, attendance from outlying areas may be sporadic. Pure assembly work does not require an extensive amount of education. In fact, I have seen many plants where the operations are broken down so that any job can be learned in fifteen minutes. However, you do need a higher level of education to perform many of the managerial, clerical, administrative, engineering and financial functions. Additionally, poorly educated personnel are prone to errors along the way. For all intents and purposes, these errors will translate into delays.

## Making Contact

How do we want to interface with our new source? There are a number of ways to go about this and a host of conditions that will go into selecting the proper procurement channel. The size of the producing company, its current level of expertise in exporting, the laws of the country, the customs of the country, the ability of personnel to communicate in English, and our ability to contact the company directly are just a few factors to consider.

If the supplier is used to dealing directly with foreign buyers and is set up to do so, there is no reason for us not to contact the supplier ourselves. This will be less expensive than working with a host of intermediaries. (The least expensive, of course, would be for us to work with a subsidiary here in this country). We still need to plan on a visit ourselves. If we would not buy from an American supplier without a quality survey, it makes less sense to do so with offshore suppliers. Besides if we are going to establish a relationship, nothing beats a face-to-face meeting.

We may be able to use one of our own divisions in that country to do some of the legwork for us, such as surveying the plant, performing a quality audit, gathering financial and technical data, starting the negotiation process, handling the negotiations, monitoring schedules and/or milestones, and assisting with paperwork and even payments.

If the procurement is a large one and we intend to buy many different items in that country over a long period of time, we may want to set up an IPO (International Procurement Office). Having our own buying office will allow us to have daily communication, periodic meetings, on-site problem resolution, and facilitate most of the ongoing interchange that will need to take place. The main weakness of an IPO is its inability to help with design.

In the event that we need to work with a third party there are a whole host of intermediaries, or "middlemen," we can turn to for help in arranging this procurement. There are import houses, commission houses, trading companies, subsidiaries, agents, import brokers, not to mention the embassies and agencies of the countries involved.

## Customs and Linguistic Differences

Around the world every country has customs which differ from ours. I can tell you from first hand experience that in many cases we have earned the title of "Ugly American." I have seen far too many people try to deal with people in other nations in the same way they deal with people here. They are brash, demanding, rude and not only insensitive to the feelings and customs of others, but even ignorant and intolerant of the differences. It is important to remember that indirectly we represent our country, as well as our company.

Often it is out of ignorance that we offend someone else. An old colleague of mine told of his trip on a trade mission to Japan many years ago. He and his wife met with some very influential Japanese. One night the Japanese hosted a dinner for them in one of their finer restaurants. They were served a number of Japanese "delicacies" that the Americans would not normally eat. Trying very hard not to insult their hosts, he and his wife dutifully and graciously tasted everything, no matter how unappetizing they thought it was. At the end of the meal, plates of fruit were served. Still somewhat hungry, my colleague quickly put a few grapes in his mouth and horrified his hosts. The Japanese would not think of eating fruit that had not been peeled.

Here are just a few of the differences you may encounter.

**All Business.** As Americans, we tend to dive right in; we want to get down to business as quickly as possible. Many cultures want to first take care of social amenities. The foreign businessmen may want to find out more about us and our companies before they are willing to sit down and do business. They may want to know about our families, our pets and even our hobbies. Many of them will want to understand us better and know more about who they are dealing with. We need to be aware of this and allow time for this to happen. Sometimes it will take days before we can get down to or conclude the business at hand.

**Decisions.** In some countries decisions are made from the top down, and in some countries they are made from the bottom up. In other countries decisions are made by consensus. It is important for us to make sure we know exactly who we are meeting with and whether or not they are the decision-makers. In many cases they will be fact finders. Two questions that we should always seek answers to are:

- Who will make the decision?
- How will it be made?

One common mistake that is often made is interpreting the word "yes." As Americans, we take "yes" as a sign of agreement. In other cultures you will find that "yes" means "I understand." The person may not necessarily agree to what has been discussed.

**Meetings.** If the people you meet with do not speak English, make sure you bring your own interpreter. That is the only way you will know for certain what was said. Not only is it a matter of how much trust you can give an interpreter who is in the employ of the other side. Your own interpreter would be able to give you an understanding of any side discussions that may occur, whereas the supplier's interpreter would ignore these.

Also, be sure to take notes and write down any agreements that were made, important points that were discussed, and what the next steps are. Make sure the supplier's representatives agree.

**Gestures.** Simple gestures that are acceptable in the United States may have some very different meanings in other countries. The OK sign (thumb and index finger in a circle) is considered obscene and rude in many countries. In Middle Eastern countries, never offer anything with your left hand (as the left hand is used for bathroom hygiene) and never show anyone the bottoms of your shoes.

**Language.** Since many times the suppliers will not speak English, try not to use slang or colloquial phrases as they are more difficult to interpret. Even if the supplier does speak English, be sure to speak slowly and clearly, avoiding slang or colloquial phrases, as that will lessen the opportunities for misinterpretation and also help tone down the stereotype that all Americans are aggressive. Also, avoid jokes; they do not translate well due to differences in humor from one country to the next.

**Power.** In some countries you will find the supplier will want to impress you by demonstrating the amount of power he holds and can wield over the local government or other organizations. Since we are not used to such displays we tend to react poorly. If we were more culturally attuned we would view them in a different light.

**Gifts.** Gift giving is prohibited in many countries, and, at the same time, in many countries it is part of the getting acquainted process. Some countries will have extensive rituals associated with the giving of gifts. A good idea is to follow the lead of your host. In all cases make sure you know what is considered suitable. You should also know when flowers and thank you notes are appropriate.

This gives you an idea of what you will have to learn. My advice, however, is to learn as much as possible about the customs of any country before attempting to do business there, especially those customs related to conducting business. One of the most important things to learn would be to find out about any absolute "faux pas," things you never do because they will kill a deal and/or a relationship. I also think it is a good idea to learn more about a country's history and geography so as not to appear ignorant.

We do indeed have a different mentality, and we definitely do approach our business dealings differently. And, yes, we are the buyers, but that does not give us the right to expect that everyone should adapt to our customs, beliefs and value system. The more we insist on doing it our way, the more suppliers will want to introduce intermediaries to deal with us. And remember, every person that enters the chain adds cost.

## Logistics and Time Considerations

**Time Difference.** Remember that there are significant time differences between the United States and other parts of the world. This makes communication a problem, especially if your suppliers do not speak English. Many times we will have to make calls from home at odd hours. Due to time differences, it may already be "tomorrow" for our suppliers when we talk to them. Often you will have to fax messages back and forth, which takes away from the give and take of a conversation.

Each country has its own holidays that it celebrates, as well as different periods when most vacations are taken. For example, there are parts of Europe that shut down for the month of August. We need to know what these holidays and "down times" are in each country in which we conduct business. That way we can avoid any surprise delays.

**Distance.** The distance to a supplier needs to be taken into account when we need to visit and when goods are shipped. A quality survey on the other side of the world is a considerably more expensive trip than a 20 mile drive from our plant or even a two hour domestic flight. Freight costs will definitely increase because of the distance. Duties, tariffs and taxes need to be consider. We need to plan for the delays associated with customs on both sides. We will want to make sure we know the true landed cost for an item so we can accurately measure the success of the procurement.

**Logistics.** We will want to be very clear as to who is handling the logistics of getting products out of one country and into ours. We may share this responsibility as long as all of the bases are covered. It will be important that we understand the meanings of "Incoterms," the internationally recognized standard definitions, prepared by the International Chamber of Commerce in 1936, that define the buyers' and sellers' responsibilities.

**Managing Global Suppliers.** This can be a difficult task, but it doesn't have to be. It is really no different than managing domestic suppliers; it just requires more effort. Just as with a domestic supplier, we need a system for measuring supplier performance, as well as a feedback mechanism to make sure the supplier is aware of the results. We will want to keep up the pressure on containing costs and should be working with the foreign supplier to accomplish these goals as we would with any domestic supplier. The area we have to work on is managing the relationship, if we are expecting it to be a long-term venture with a supplier we want to cultivate. The ongoing communication that is required is a little bit harder to achieve, but not overly difficult. If this is a spot commodity buy, however, managing the relationship is not as important an issue.

## Legal and Social Considerations

Whose law will govern? In the United States we have

the UCC (Uniform Commercial Code) which takes precedence in case of disputes, probably negating all of that legalese we put on the back of our purchase orders and acknowledgments. The U.S. has signed the CISG (Convention on the International Sale of Goods) prepared by the United Nations, which unless specifically excluded will apply, possibly even in this country. While similar to the UCC, the CISG has two major differences. First, the CISG will allow verbal contracts. Second, under the CISG the buyer may not have the right to return defective goods, but may have to offer the seller the option of repairing them locally, thereby reducing overall shipping costs.

In many countries unions exist because the law requires them. They are, however, different from those in the U.S. in that they work much more closely with management. In those countries which require all manufacturing employees to be represented, the manufacturing companies must consult with the unions before any changes can be made. While we often hesitate to buy from unionized companies because of the threat of work stoppages, we should first check and see whether the law requires them.

We have all read about child labor, sweatshops, slave labor and other atrocities that exist in some offshore companies. It is up to us to be aware of the working conditions and refuse to deal with those companies that do not treat their workers well.

One last thing to be aware of: under U.S. law, under the Foreign Corrupt Practices Act, we can be found criminally liable for bribery and other illegal acts, even if they are legal in the country we committed them.

## Summary

The risks and benefits are summed up as follows.

## Risks

**Communication.** Lack of a dependable communication system inhibits the free flow of information, the ease of placing and monitoring orders, and introduces delays.

**Currency & Payment Terms.** Currencies can fluctuate widely and negate any benefits gained from cheaper labor. Payment terms vary from what we are used to in the United States.

**Language.** Different languages create definite barrier to communication and also increase the probability of miscommunication.

**Culture.** There are many cultural differences we need to be aware of. In addition to the possibility of offending, cultural differences can also lead to miscommunication.

**Legal Issues.** In the U.S. we are used to the Uniform Commercial Code. The laws of other countries need to be taken into account to adequately assess our risk. (Whose law governs? Which court will hear the suit?)

**Hidden Costs.** We need to be sure we understand what costs, above and beyond the purchase price, impact our total cost. VAT (Value Added Tax), other taxes, duties, tariffs, brokers fees, and expected or unexpected bribes, among other things, may be very different than we are used to.

## Benefits

**Quality.** Often we will find the quality from an offshore supplier is better than that we can find here in the United States.

**Market Opportunities.** As we work in other countries, we may find some market opportunities we have not yet considered. Some may be a direct result of the relationship with our new source.

**Cost Savings.** Taking advantage of cheaper labor and advanced technology should result in significant cost savings.

**Competition.** Added competition from offshore suppliers may help our local sources improve their operations.

**Technology.** Again we may find technology that is either not available domestically or more advanced than what we have in the United States.

We go offshore because we feel we can either get a better product or a better price. If we are cautious in our approach, there is no reason we cannot get excellent results from dealing with trading partners in other countries. Fear of the unknown should not stop us, but we should not dive right in without first educating ourselves.

# MEASUREMENTS

# CHAPTER NINE

## Measuring Performance

Performance measurements must be an integral part of every one of our operations, including our suppliers and their performance. Measurements force us to take a step back and assess whether we are heading in the right direction, whether we are meeting our targets, and whether or not corrective action is needed. And since our ultimate goal is customer satisfaction, we should make sure that our measurements lead us in that direction.

## The Wrong Measurements

We know that people pay more attention to things that they know will be measured. I have seen it over and over again. As soon as we start measuring something it improves. It immediately gets the attention it should have had in the first place. Conversely things that are not measured begin to fade into the background and decline. Typically, once top management has decreed the measurement, everything that was not focused on begins to deteriorate. I once worked for a Fortune 100 company where the Vice President of Manufacturing Operations told me that we had eleven objectives for the year. He said that if we did an outstanding job on ten of them and missed the sales (product out the door) objective, we failed. But if we made the sales objective, and miss the other ten objectives, we would have a partial success. Sales were probably what his bonus was tied to, and the emphasis placed on meeting the sales targets out stripped everything else.

The emphasis that he placed on making the sales caused us to spend more in other areas. We paid a lot of expediting fees. We had an extremely large FedEx bill. Our inventory levels started to climb. WIP (work-in-process) levels increased. Internal lead times increased, causing us to push more out into WIP earlier. Our internal expediting force doubled. We made the sales, but what a price we paid. We obviously had the wrong measure for success.

## Purchase Price Variance (PPV)

Some of the measurements that we have used in the past need to be reviewed to assure ourselves that we are correctly measuring and not driving ourselves in the wrong direction. For example, let's take a quick look at

Purchase Price Variance (PPV). This has long been a standard measurement in Purchasing, and our finance people always want to see it. But what does it tell us? We think it is an indication that the price we paid on the purchase order is more or less than some other price. Unfortunately we are not always sure what that other price ought to be. I have seen people use the standard cost, the average cost, the price last paid, the target (or budgeted) price, the projected standard and even the standard cost adjusted for inflation or recession.

If we talk to people who are measured on PPV, a number of things begin to become very clear.

- Buyers never like PPV because they always think the price they are varying from was never right to begin with (and they are usually right).

- Across the board adjustments are not necessarily reflective of how any particular commodity or segment of the market is doing.

- The supplier that has a price that is lower than the target will get the order over a better supplier with a higher quality product.

- The amount of paperwork for anything over the target price can be overwhelming and nonproductive.

## PPV as the Driver

If we use PPV as the primary measurement for individual buyers, we will definitely drive the buyers in the wrong direction. Buyers, knowing that their performance is being evaluated solely on PPV, will make that their primary criteria for supplier selection. A supplier who quotes the lowest price, or even just a lower price, may win the order.

The results of concentrating solely on a lower price usually means that many other costs which are not reflected in the PPV will increase. These are costs like production rework, inventory carrying costs, production delays, MRB (Material Review Board) purchase part rework, and RTS (Return To Supplier – which includes shipping costs and additional inspection costs). We also need to take into account the consumption of valuable "human" resources that were wasted on additional activities that should not have been required in the first place. Also these increased costs are not only not reflected in the PPV, they are usually found inflating someone else's budget. We are under the gun enough without bringing more negative focus on us based on the lack of quality in what we have delivered.

This does not mean we should drop PPV as measurement. It can still tell us something useful. It certainly is useful for trend information. We just need to be careful that we are not dependent on PPV as the sole measurement. And we certainly don't want to examine every variance that comes along. We should know at purchase order placement time if there is a problem. PPV at the end of the month or the quarter is the wrong time for an investigation. In fact the real way to control PPV is to have targeted cost reductions in the commodities that make up the major cost drivers for our products. In that way we have not only taken a proactive step toward creating a favorable PPV, we have also begun to give ourselves a competitive advantage in the marketplace by reducing the cost to produce our products.

## Least Total Cost

A far better measure is least total cost. Getting an item 10% cheaper is truly not less expensive when we figure out the costs associated with the additional activities required and then add them into the price paid. The PPV would quickly go in the other direction. We need to be thinking about the least cost to our company and not just what shows up in Purchasing.

The least total cost calculation should be done prior to placement of the purchase order. For example, if we get a substantial price break for a large quantity, we need to add in the cost of carrying the extra inventory to decide if it truly is the correct decision to buy the larger quantity.

## Other Key Measurements

There are a number of key measurements that we should be looking at. It is not important to use every measurement known to man. We would then spend far more time measuring and analyzing and less time doing the things that make a difference. A cost accountant I once worked with had a great sign posted on his file cabinet. It read, "The cost of counting the beans should not exceed the cost of the beans." We need to make sure we are getting enough quality information from our measurements so we can use it to make better, quicker and more effective buying and selection decisions. Some other possible measurements related to our suppliers are:

- supplier performance ratings.
- number of past due orders per supplier.
- delivery performance.
- quoted lead times versus actual delivery times.
- percentage of shipments to stock and WIP.

## Supplier Performance Ratings

A good supplier rating system should contain the following elements. I've taken the liberty of adding some suggested point values to each one.

| Acceptable Lots | 15 points |
|---|---|
| Certified Supplier | 20 points |
| Support Documentation | 10 points |
| Quantity Correct | 5 points |
| On-Time Delivery | 20 points |
| Total Cost | 20 points |
| Customer Service | 10 points |

These add to a possible 100 points that a supplier can earn. Keep in mind that these are only suggestions. Depending on how we view our business we are free to adjust the point value to one that makes sense for our business. There are some adjustment factors that I would like to throw in. A supplied item that fails after being incorporated into my product is a big mistake. A supplied item that fails after I've shipped the product is even worse. The cost of both these events is significant. There-fore, we should take into consideration the following occurrences when awarding points and subtract them accordingly.

| | |
|---|---|
| Production Failures | -15 points |
| Field Failures | -20 points |

It is important to agree on an objective way of award-ing the points, so that they are awarded consistently for all suppliers. It will also mean that there can be no arguments as to the final ratings as all concerned will have agreed on the methodology to be used. Let's look at the seven elements individually.

**Acceptable Lots**. If a lot is not acceptable does the supplier lose all 15 points? Is it penalized 5 points for each lot that fails? Is the point value based on a percent-age? (8 acceptable lots out of 10 = 80% times 15 points = 12 points.) This will give you some insight as to how many ways you can calculate the same measurement. The key to success is that we agree and that we are consistent. Even a wrong measure measured consistently will give you trend information.

**Certified Supplier**. 20 points for being a certified supplier. How many points for being in pursuit of certi-fication? 5 points for each phase of certification?

**Support Documentation**. 10 points for having all the required documentation arrive with the parts. Cer-tificates of compliance, test data, lot control data, process control charts, etc.

**Quantity Correct.** 5 points for the quantity required, no more, no less. Is there a tolerance? 1%? 2%?

**On-Time Delivery.** 20 points for on-time delivery. Is there a tolerance? 2 days early and no days late?

**Total Cost.** 20 points. We discussed least total cost earlier. Costs should be as expected. If parts require extra inspection, rework, additional testing, or anything else that adds cost, we should be looking at subtracting points from the maximum number of points which may be awarded.

**Customer Service.** 10 points for good customer service. This is usually subjective. Sometimes good customer service from a supplier means tickets to the ball game or lunch with the salesman. We need to be sure that we have an objective way of measuring customer service and that everyone agrees on what the points will be awarded for. This way there is no argument.

For example: If I call the supplier and get an answering machine, no points are awarded. If I call the supplier and get someone who doesn't know who I am and doesn't know who how to direct my call, no points are awarded. I begin to award points when I reach someone who knows: who I am, what I buy, how I use his company's product, what I produce, and where I might have trouble. Points could be earned if the person knows how to help me and how to get me what I need in a timely manner. I might assign points for technical assistance during development, suggestions for improvements, or any other service that I consider part of my success. Remember, in

| Elements | Max. Pts. | Months | | | | | | | | | | | |
|---|---|---|---|---|---|---|---|---|---|---|---|---|---|
| | | 1 | 2 | 3 | 4 | 5 | 6 | 7 | 8 | 9 | 10 | 11 | 12 |
| Certification | 10 | | | | | | | | | | | | |
| Product Quality | 25 | | | | | | | | | | | | |
| Delivery Performance | 30 | | | | | | | | | | | | |
| Cost Performance | 15 | | | | | | | | | | | | |
| Cooperation | 10 | | | | | | | | | | | | |
| Quantity | 10 | | | | | | | | | | | | |
| Totals | 100 | | | | | | | | | | | | |
| % of Business | | | | | | | | | | | | | |

*Figure 9.1*

order to be objective, we need to be consistent in award-
ing points to suppliers.

## Supplier Yearly Performance Summary

Once we have the data for a supplier rating system
we should put it into a summary chart similar to the one
in Figure 9.1. That way we will be able to see trend data
and understand whether a supplier's overall rating is
getting better or worse. Another important aspect of
trends is the comparison of two possible sources. Consider the ratings of two suppliers of the same product.
Supplier A's ratings for the last three months are 85, 81
and 79. Supplier B's ratings for the last three months are
50, 55 and 70. Which supplier would we prefer? Supplier
A's ratings are on the decline. Instead of working toward
improving its ratings, it is actually going in the wrong
direction, which may be a symptom of more serious
problems. Supplier B, on the other hand, has put in place
a continuous improvement program and is proactively,
aggressively and successfully improving its business
and its ratings. I might be inclined to support Supplier B
in its quest for excellence. Supplier B would be worth
cultivating and nurturing since it is the type of supplier we
are seeking, even though its ratings were low to start with.

## Concerns on Developing a Supplier Rating System

Supplier rating systems are one of those systems that
never seem to satisfy everyone. A rating system project
usually extends in time because it is so difficult for

everyone to agree with. The arguing feels like it goes on forever. Used incorrectly, the system will not yield the long awaited benefits we are looking for.

We should make sure we:

- use a cross-functional team approach when developing our program. That way everyone will have input and, therefore, buy-in, which should eliminate focusing on the numbers instead of the problems they represent.

- use quantifiable data. Having the team decide ahead of time exactly how the points will be awarded makes rating objective and not subjective. And again, we need to eliminate the focus on the numbers; we should be concentrating on solving problems.

- present the system to our suppliers before we begin to rate them. That let's them know what is coming. (There should be no surprises here, we do not want to have an adversarial relationship with our suppliers.) This also gives them an opportunity to critique the process and perhaps make some suggestions that will improve it. Also we should be prepared for them to tell us whether or not we are good customers.

- use the ratings as kind of a report card and coach our suppliers with ways to improve their performance. Our goal is not to punish the suppliers. Our goal is a steady, dependable stream of quality materials.

We should be careful about:

- using subjective data. There is always a way to quantify something. Using subjective data will only increase the arguments over where the numbers came from and how they were calculated.

- developing the rating system in a vacuum. What we purchase affects all areas of the company. Cross-functional consensus is a key to success. I used to work for a company that had suppliers that were rated as being 98% on time, yet more than half of the jobs on the shop floor had shortages, not to mention the kits we couldn't release because of missing material.

- rating our suppliers without them knowing what we are going to do and how we intend to go about it. Everyone wants to know how they will be measured.

- using a mass mailing to notify suppliers. We should be able to find a way to do it on a more personal level, especially with our key suppliers.

- using the tool to beat up suppliers. That is not the way to nurture the relationship. Remember our goal is a long term relationship with quality suppliers.

Supplier performance rating systems are good to put in place but may have a short life. If we are really going after a partnering relationship, the ratings should be unnecessary. The performance of certified suppliers usually speaks for itself. An excellent supplier is one that measures himself and tells us what his performance rating is in relation to the items that he supplies us. And if that rating is less than expected, he would also be prepared to show us what he is putting in place to remedy the situation.

## Past Due Orders

The number of past due orders per supplier should be an absolute number. It really doesn't matter if it is one of one, one of ten, or one of fifty. If the parts are not here when I need them, my costs begin to go up and my customer service levels begin to go down.

## Delivery Performance

The closer we get to Just-In-Time, which is the real measure of efficiency, the more important delivery performance becomes. In the ideal world I want to receive the parts today that I am going to use in production tomorrow. In fact in some industries, such as the automotive industry, we are beginning to see deliveries scheduled to the line more than once a day. In these instances there is no tolerance. Early is just as bad as late.

## Quoted Lead Times Versus Actual Delivery Times

This measurement will help eliminate suppliers who tell us what they think we want to hear in order to get the order. The more "padding" we take out of our schedules the more we rely on the dependability of our suppliers. It will also help us identify those suppliers whose processes are not predictable, and, therefore, their quoted lead times are not accurate.

## Percentage Of Shipments Directly To Stock and WIP

**Percentage of Shipments Directly to Stock.** This figure is derived by taking the number of shipments that do not have to be inspected by us and dividing that by the number of shipments received. Monitoring and improving this measurement will allow us to eliminate inspection costs as well as reduce our inventory carrying costs.

**Percentage of Shipments Directly to WIP.** This figure is derived by taking the number of shipments that can be delivered directly to WIP and dividing that by the number of shipments received. Monitoring and improving this measurement will give us the cost savings above and also eliminate the costs associated with stocking the materials.

Both of these measurements are indicators of how well we are doing in our partnering relationships. Our ultimate goal is a shift from Ship-to-Stock to Ship-to-WIP.

# CASE STUDY

## CHAPTER TEN

Chapter Four introduced the Material Positioning Matrix. It is important to actually go through an example of how to use this tool. Utilizing the thought process necessary to effectively use the tool will help us appreciate its value and also make sure we have truly added it to our toolbox. I encourage each of you to get a small cross-functional group together and go through the exercise together.

For the purpose of this exercise, let's assume that our product is small motors. Motor technology has not changed much in recent years. A motor consists of a casing, a shaft, a ball bearing, a winding, and some magnets. We will choose magnets as our commodity. Having selected the product and the material or com-

# INFLUENCE ON COMPANY RESULTS

**MATERIAL/COMMODITY:** ___Magnets___

| | A | B | C |
|---|---|---|---|
| | **Market Success Relative Weight** | **Influence of Material (Scale 0-5)** | **Weighted Influence (A x B)** |
| **COST**<br>World Pricing<br>Domestic Pricing<br>Cost of Inventory<br>Activity Based Costing<br>Total Cost Management<br>Etc. | .5 | ___ | ___ |
| **QUALITY**<br>Product Quality<br>Service Quality<br>Reliability<br>Etc. | .3 | ___ | ___ |
| **TIME**<br>Long-term Agreements<br>Flexibility<br>Short Lead Times<br>Freight Terms<br>Etc. | .1 | ___ | ___ |
| **TECHNOLOGY**<br>Commodity Leader<br>Market Position<br>Equipment<br>Processes<br>Innovations<br>Vision (Future)<br>Etc. | .1 | ___ | ___ |
| **Total** | 1.0 | **Sum of C's** ___<br>**=Influence**<br>**Index** ___ | |

*Figure 10.1*

modity the next step is determining the influence on our company's results.

## Calculating the Influence on Company Results

In Figure 10.1, we use Column A to assess the reasons for our success in the marketplace. Our differentiator in the marketplace appears to be primarily cost. Our motors are less expensive than the competition's for comparable quality. Therefore, we will give the cost element a value of .5 (or 50% of the allowable value). Our next consideration is quality. The quality of our motors is a little better than the competition in our price range. So quality becomes the second influence on our success, but not to the extent that price is. Therefore we will award quality a value of .3. The influence of the time element is negligible and rates a value of .1. Time is important, but the time element for our product is no different than the time elements of our competitors'. And as I mentioned before the technology has not changed much over time and is not much different than the competition's. Therefore, it also rates a value of .1. Remember, the values in Column A must add up to 1.0.

We use Column B to assess the influence of the chosen commodity or material on our market success factors. We have chosen magnets as the material we are evaluating. The magnets are a cost driver, and, therefore, have a significant influence on the cost of our product. In Figure 10.2, we award the magnets a value of 4 (out of 5) for their influence. Magnets do come in different quali-

# INFLUENCE ON COMPANY RESULTS

**MATERIAL/COMMODITY:** _Magnets_

| | A<br>**Market Success Relative Weight** | B<br>**Influence of Material (Scale 0-5)** | C<br>**Weighted Influence (A x B)** |
|---|---|---|---|
| **COST**<br>World Pricing<br>Domestic Pricing<br>Cost of Inventory<br>Activity Based Costing<br>Total Cost Management<br>Etc. | .5 | 4 | |
| **QUALITY**<br>Product Quality<br>Service Quality<br>Reliability<br>Etc. | .3 | 3 | |
| **TIME**<br>Long-term Agreements<br>Flexibility<br>Short Lead Times<br>Freight Terms<br>Etc. | .1 | 2 | |
| **TECHNOLOGY**<br>Commodity Leader<br>Market Position<br>Equipment<br>Processes<br>Innovations<br>Vision (Future)<br>Etc. | .1 | 2 | |
| **Total** | 1.0 | **Sum of C's** _____<br>**=Influence Index** _____ | |

*Figure 10.2*

ties, which affect the reliability of our product. Their influence on the quality element is not as great as their influence on cost. We give the magnets a value of 3 for their influence on quality. Our ability to get the magnets in a timely manner allows us to meet the same time frames as our competition. We can award the magnets a value of 2 for the time element. And lastly, for the technology element, we have also awarded a value of 2, again because the technology has not changed much over time and is not much different than the competition's.

Column C shows us the weighted influence of the commodity on our success in the marketplace. We multiply the values in Column A by the values in Column B and enter them in Column C, as shown in Figure 10.3. The sum of the values in Column C gives us our influence index – 3.3. This will be plotted against the Y-axis, *Influence on Company Results*, of the matrix in Figure 10.5.

## Calculating Procurement Risk

We will use the chart in Figure 10.4 to calculate procurement risk. Our first value is for Bargaining Power. There are not as many suppliers as we would like to see that produce the precision magnets we use. We do not have a lot of choice in changing to something else. On a scale of 0-5, we therefore award a 4, indicating the seller has the Bargaining Power, at least in the short term.

The next element is Substitution. The cost of switching to a different material is higher than we would like for ease of switching and would include a lot of research and development. We would be willing to switch if

# INFLUENCE ON COMPANY RESULTS

MATERIAL/COMMODITY: ___Magnets___

| | A | B | C |
|---|---|---|---|
| | **Market Success Relative Weight** | **Influence of Material (Scale 0-5)** | **Weighted Influence (A x B)** |
| **COST**<br>World Pricing<br>Domestic Pricing<br>Cost of Inventory<br>Activity Based Costing<br>Total Cost Management<br>Etc. | .5 | 4 | 2.0 |
| **QUALITY**<br>Product Quality<br>Service Quality<br>Reliability<br>Etc. | .3 | 3 | .9 |
| **TIME**<br>Long-term Agreements<br>Flexibility<br>Short Lead Times<br>Freight Terms<br>Etc. | .1 | 2 | .2 |
| **TECHNOLOGY**<br>Commodity Leader<br>Market Position<br>Equipment<br>Processes<br>Innovations<br>Vision (Future)<br>Etc. | .1 | 2 | .2 |
| | | **Sum of C's** | 3.3 |
| **Total** | 1.0 | **=Influence Index** | 3.3 |

*Figure 10.3*

# PROCUREMENT RISK

MATERIAL /COMMODITY _____Magnets_____

|  |  | Procurement Risk (Scale 0-5) |
|---|---|---|

**BARGAINING POWER**
_____

| buyer | | | | | seller | 4 |
|---|---|---|---|---|---|---|
| 0 | 1 | 2 | 3 | 4 | 5 | |

_____

**SUBSTITUTION**
_____

| easy | | | | difficult | | 2 |
|---|---|---|---|---|---|---|
| 0 | 1 | 2 | 3 | 4 | 5 | |

_____

**RIVALRY**
_____

| intense | | | | | mild | 2 |
|---|---|---|---|---|---|---|
| 0 | 1 | 2 | 3 | 4 | 5 | |

_____

**BARRIERS**
_____

| weak | | | | | strong | 1 |
|---|---|---|---|---|---|---|
| 0 | 1 | 2 | 3 | 4 | 5 | |

_____

9
___

SUM/4 =   2.2
RISK
INDEX

*Figure 10.4*

someone came along with a better magnet. We have therefore awarded a value of 2 for Substitution.

The third element to consider is Rivalry. There are enough companies that do make magnets for many other uses that we are pretty confident we would be able to find other sources if the current sources were to go out of business or become too costly. We therefore awarded a value of 2 for Rivalry.

There are few Barriers to the magnet business: it is not really capital intensive, raw materials are readily available, there is not a lot of government regulation, and many of the patents have long since expired. Ease of entry into the magnet business would not be that difficult. We could even do it ourselves, if necessary. We therefore award a value of 1 to Entry Barriers.

We then add the four values and divide by 4 to give us the Risk Index. Our Risk Index in this case is 9 divided by 4, which is 2.2. This is our second coordinate and will be plotted along the X-axis, *Procurement Risk*, of the matrix in Figure 10.5.

Figure 10.5 indicates that there is a relatively high influence on company results with not as much procurement risk. Magnets fall into the *Leverage Components* quadrant of our matrix.

We would then go to our strategy matrix, Figure 10.6, to select the strategy(s) that make sense in our circumstances. As you can see almost all of the strategies can be effective in more than one of the quadrants.

## MATERIAL POSITIONING MATRIX

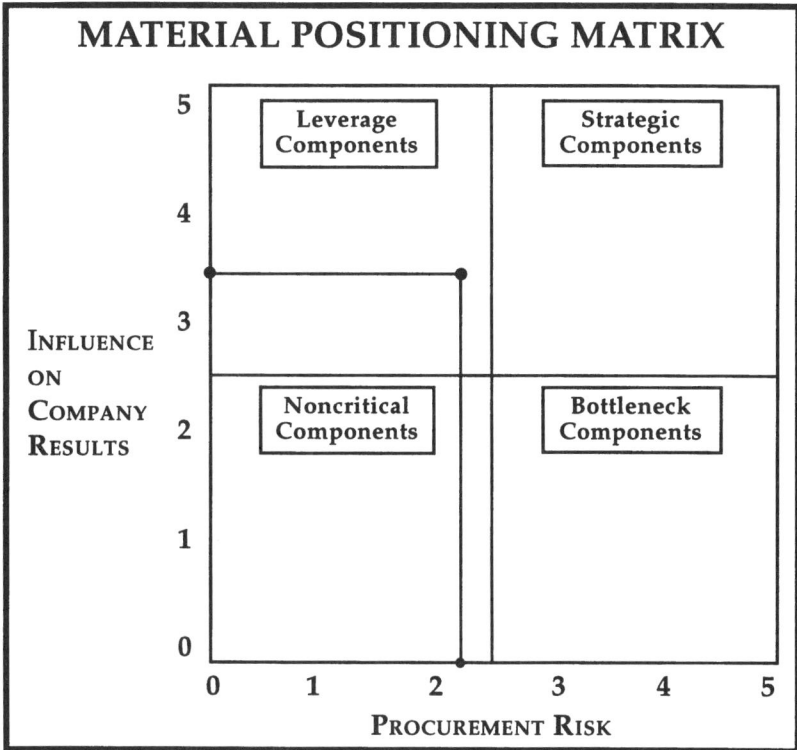

*Figure 10.5*

Additionally, we have not carried our calculations to many decimal places, nor is the grid mutually exclusive. Our coordinates do not plot too far from the edges of the next quadrant, and therefore strategies from that quadrant may be also be applicable. The matrix, therefore, is only a guide as to where to begin. We would begin by first examining those strategies that are usually found to be effective for Leveraged Components. The particular circumstances will differ for each company, each commodity and the status of each procurement. The cross-functional team will choose the appropriate strategy(s).

## STRATEGY MATRIX

| | STRATEGIC | LEVERAGE | BOTTLENECK | NONCRITICAL |
|---|---|---|---|---|
| Partner/Alliance | X | | | |
| Cultivating Suppliers | X | X | X | |
| Long-Term Agreement/Contract | X | X | X | X |
| Standardize | X | X | X | X |
| Quality Improvement | X | X | | |
| Overhead Cost Reduction | X | X | | X |
| Consolidate With Other Divisions | | X | | X |
| Competitive Bidding | | X | | X |
| Price Rollback | | X | | X |
| Supplier Reduction | | X | | X |
| Cross Commodity Leveraging | | X | X | X |
| Internal Price Benchmarking | | X | X | X |
| Re-source to New Suppliers | | | X | |
| Substitute | | | X | |

*Figure 10.6*

Having agreed on the strategy(s), the team will be expected to support the strategies and make them work.

One final note. As the world changes so do the strategies and the tools. The tools can be updated to suit our current status. If, for example, we feel that the elements of risk have changed, we can update the model to adapt to those changes. Likewise if we feel the influence in the marketplace calls for the elements to be further stratified, again the model should be changed to accommodate those changes. However, care should be taken not to destroy the integrity of the model.

Good Luck!!

# RESOURCE
# GUIDE

## ADDITIONAL PURCHASING RESOURCES
## FROM PT PUBLICATIONS, INC.

3109 45th Street, Suite 100
West Palm Beach, FL 33407-1915
**1-800-547-4326**

### THE PURCHASING ENCYCLOPEDIA

*Just-In-Time Purchasing: In Pursuit of Excellence*          $29.95
  Peter L. Grieco, Jr., Michael W. Gozzo
  & Jerry W. Claunch

| | |
|---|---|
| *Glossary of Key Purchasing Terms, Acronyms,* <br> *and Formulas* <br> PT Publications | $14.95 |
| *Supplier Certification II: A Handbook for* <br> *Achieving Excellence through Continuous Improvement* <br> Peter L. Grieco, Jr. | $49.95 |
| *World Class: Measuring Its Achievement* <br> Peter L. Grieco, Jr. | $39.95 |
| *Purchasing Performance Measurements: A Roadmap* <br> *For Excellence* <br> Mel Pilachowski | $12.95 |
| *The World Of Negotiations: Never Being a Loser* <br> Peter L. Grieco, Jr. and Paul G. Hine | $39.95 |
| *How To Conduct Supplier Surveys and Audits* <br> Janet L. Przirembel | $14.95 |
| *Supply Management Toolbox: How to Manage* <br> *Your Suppliers* <br> Peter L. Grieco, Jr. | $26.95 |
| *Purchasing Capital Equipment* <br> Wayne L. Douchkoff | $14.95 |
| *Power Purchasing: Supply Management in* <br> *in the 21st Century* <br> Peter L. Grieco, Jr. and Carl R. Cooper | $39.95 |
| *Global Sourcing* <br> Lee Krotseng | $14.95 |
| *Purchasing Contract Law, UCC, and Patents* <br> Mark Grieco | $14.95 |
| *EDI Purchasing: The Electronic Gateway* <br> *to the Future* <br> Steven Marks | $14.95 |
| *Leasing Smart* <br> Craig A. Melby and Jane Utzman | $14.95 |
| *Supplier Selection* <br> Judith A. Stimson | $14.95 |
| *MRO Purchasing* <br> Peter L. Grieco, Jr. | $14.95 |

| | |
|---|---|
| *Purchasing Transportation* | $14.95 |
| Charles L. Perry | |
| *Procurement Reengineering* | $14.95 |
| Ben H. Laaper | |
| *Purchasing Ethics* | $14.95 |
| Peter L. Grieco, Jr. | |
| *Supplier Strategies* | $14.95 |
| Charles Goldfeld | |
| *Supplier Partnerships* | $14.95 |
| Judith A. Stimson | |
| *The Complete Guide to Contracts Management For* | $18.95 |
| *Facilities Services* | |
| John P. Mahoney and Linda S. Keckler | |

## PURCHASING VIDEO EDUCATION SERIES

*Supplier Certification The Path to Excellence*

| | |
|---|---|
| Tape 1: Why Supplier Certification? | $395.00 |
| Tape 2: Quality at the Supplier | $395.00 |
| Tape 3: How to Select a Supplier | $395.00 |
| Tape 4: Supplier Surveys and Audits | $395.00 |
| Tape 5: Supplier Quality Agreements | $395.00 |
| Tape 6: Supplier Ratings | $395.00 |
| Tape 7: Phases of Supplier Certification | $395.00 |
| Tape 8: Implementing a Supplier Cert. Program | $395.00 |
| Tape 9: Evaluating Your Supplier Cert. Program | $395.00 |
| | |
| Complete Nine Tape Series | $1,995.00 |

## PURCHASING AUDIO TAPES

| | |
|---|---|
| *The World of Negotiations: How to Win Every Time* | $39.95 |

## PURCHASING SOFTWARE

*Supplier Survey and Audit Software*      $395.00
   Developed by  Professionals For Technology, Inc.

## ADDITIONAL PROFESSIONAL TEXTBOOKS

*Failure Modes and Effects Analysis: Predicting*    $39.95
   *and Preventing Problems Before They Occur*
   Paul Palady
*Made In America: The Total Business Concept*    $29.95
   Peter L. Grieco, Jr. and Michael W. Gozzo
*Reengineering Through Cycle Time Management*    $39.95
   Wayne L. Douchkoff and Thomas E. Petroski
*Behind Bars: Bar Coding Principles and Applications*    $39.95
   Peter L. Grieco, Jr., Michael W. Gozzo and C.J. Long
*People Empowerment: Achieving Success from Involvement*  $39.95
   Michael W. Gozzo and Wayne L. Douchkoff
*Activity Based Costing: The Key to World Class Performance* $18.00
   Peter L. Grieco, Jr. and Mel Pilachowski

# Index

## A
Acceptable lots 135
Audits 73, 84, 92

## B
Background and documentation 83-88
Banking and financial services when sourcing overseas 116
Barriers 41, 54, 56, 149, 150
Bargaining power 41, 54-55, 147, 149
Bottleneck components 43-44, 58, 95, 108, 151, 152
Bill of Material 73, 101
Bribes 126
Business knowledge 75

# C

Certified supplier *(see also supplier certification)* 135
Commitment 84, 92
Commodity teams 22-23, 59-60, 61,63
Communication 36-37, 81, 91,
Communications system when sourcing overseas 116, 126
Competition when sourcing overseas 127
Competitive bidding 58, 95, 103, 152
Competitive pricing 11
Compliance of materials 73
Compliance to regulations 76
Confidentiality 82, 91
Consolidate with other divisions 58, 95, 102-103, 152
Contingency planning 13-14
Convention on the International Sale of Goods (CISG) 124-125
Corrective action 71, 72, 73, 84, 86, 88, 89, 129
Cost 45, 48, 50, 52, 87, 144, 145, 146, 148
Cost controls 74-75
Cost reduction 97
Cost reduction goals 30-31, 83, 91
Cost savings when sourcing overseas 127
Country climate 114-117
Cross-functional team 46-47, 59-60, 61, 63, 139
Cross commodity leveraging 58, 95, 105-106, 152
Cultivating suppliers 58, 95, 97-98152
Cultural differences when sourcing overseas 119-121, 126
Currency and payment terms when sourcing overseas 126
Customer service 29, 67, 83
Customs differences when sourcing overseas 119-121
Cycle time reductions 101

# D

Data, quantifiable 139
Data, subjective 139
Decision making 120
Delivery performance 141
Department of Defense (DOD) 104
Design capability 81
Design of Experiments (DOE) 68
Detail formulation 84, 89-91
Dichotomy 10
Displays of power, when sourcing overseas 121
Distance considerations when sourcing overseas 123
Distribution process control 66
Document control processes 73
Duties 123

# E

Early Supplier Involvement (ESI) 81, 82
Easier sourcing 80
Education and training support 36
Emerging technology 29, 83
Efficient producer 32, 83
Elements of market success 49-50
Employee empowerment 77
Engineering 86
Environmental Protection Agency 76
Equal Employment Opportunity Commission 76
Ethics 76

# F

Facilities management 75
Failure Modes and Effects Analysis (FMEA) 68

Finance 86
Financial stability 27, 74, 83, 86
Force Majeure 91
Foreign Corrupt Practices Act

## G
Gages 88
Galvin, Robert 27-28
Gestures, concerns with when sourcing overseas 121
Gift giving when sourcing overseas 122
Global sourcing 111-127
    risks of 125
    benefits of 125-126
Goals 23

## H
Honesty 81

## I
Improved profitability 81-82
"Incoterms" 124
Industry knowledge 75
Influence on company  results 40-61, 144, 146-147, 148
Inspection 72
Interest in success 30, 83
Integrity 81
Internal framework 115-116
Internal price benchmarking 58, 95, 106-107, 152
International Chamber of Commerce 124
International Procurement Office (IPO) 118
ISO 9000 64

# L

Labor relations 77
Language differences when sourcing overseas 116,119,
    121, 126
Lead time 32-33, 83, 141
Least total cost 82, 103, 106, 133, 136
Legal concerns when sourcing overseas 124-125, 126
Leverage 37
Leverage components 42, 58, 95, 150, 151,152
Logistics 77-78
Logistics when sourcing overseas 116, 123-124
Long-term agreement/contract 58, 95, 98, 152
Long-term relationship 80
Loyalty 81

# M

Maintenance 69, 75, 84, 92
Management commitment 69-70
Managing global suppliers 124
Manufacturing process capability 69
Manufacturing process control 68-69
Market opportunities when sourcing overseas 127
Material Positioning Matrix 6, 39-62, 65, 79,143, 151
Material Review Board (MRB) 86, 132
Mean Time Between Failures (MTBF)
Measurements 6, 129-142
    the wrong 129-130
Meeting with overseas suppliers 121
Motorola 27-28, 29
MRO supplies 4
Mutually acceptable specifications 81

# N
Noncritical components 42, 58, 95, 151,152

# O
Occupational Safety and Health Administration 76
Offshore sourcing, reasons for 112-114
On-time delivery 136
Overhead cost reduction 58, 95, 100-102, 152

# P
Partner/Alliance 58, 94-94, 152
Partner candidate, characteristics of 82-83
Partner methodology *see Strategic partner methodology*
Partnership agreement 90-91
Past due orders 141
Personnel concerns when sourcing overseas 117
Predictability 35
Performance monitoring 73, 87
Political volatility 114-115
Predictive maintenance 75
Preventive maintenance 69, 75, 87
Product Warranty and Reliability 68
Price rollback 58, 95, 105, 152
Process evaluation 84, 88-89
Process mapping 100
Procurement risk 5, 13,40-44, 53-57, 108-109, 147, 149-150
Purchase price variance (PPV) 130-133
Purchasing council 103

# Q
Quality 45, 48, 50, 52, 86, 87, 144, 145, 146, 147, 148
Quality improvement 58, 95, 99-100, 152

Quality management 27, 72, 83
Quality system 70-71
Quality system deployment 28, 83
Quantity correct 135

**R**

Reducing the supplier base 9-24
    Benefits of 14-16
    Goals 23-24
    How large a reduction? 16-17
    What is involved? 17-21
Reliable performance 82
Re-source to new suppliers 58, 95, 107-108, 152
Return to supplier (RTS) 132
Risk factors 13
Rivalry 41, 54, 56, 149, 150

**S**

Sampling 72, 73
Self-measurement 31-32, 83
Service 85-86
Ship-to-stock 142
Ship-to-WIP 142
Shorter lead times 32-33, 83
Single-sourcing 11, 80-81, 104
Six Sigma 27-28,29
Social concerns when sourcing overseas 124-125
Sole-sourcing 11
Standardize 58, 95, 98-99, 152
Statistical methodologies 73
Statistical process control 68
Steering committee 22-23

Strategic components 44, 58, 95, 151,152
Strategic partner methodology 79-92
       stages of 83-92
Strategic plan 2, 5
Strategy Matrix 58, 94-109, 152
Substitution 41, 54, 56, 58, 95, 108-109, 147, 149, 152
Summary Commodity Listing 19
Supplier certification 5, 25-38
    Benefits to the supplier 34-37
Supplier improvement programs 82
Supplier performance ratings 134-136, 140
Supplier rating system, concerns on developing 138-140
Supplier reduction 58, 95, 105, 152
Supplier selection criteria 65-78
Supplier selection strategies 63-78, 93-109
Supplier yearly performance summary 134-136
Support documentation 135
Survey results 88
Surveys 73

**T**
Tariffs 123, 126
Taxes 123, 126
Technical support 30,35-36, 74, 82, 83
Technology 45, 48, 50, 53, 112, 127,  144, 145, 146, 147, 148
Time 45, 48, 50, 52,  144, 145, 146, 147, 148
Time difference when sourcing overseas 123
Tooling 88
Total cost 136
Transportation system when sourcing overseas 116
Trust 81

# U

Uniform Commercial Code (UCC) 40, 124-125, 126
Unions 77, 125
United Nations 124

# V

Value Added Tax 126

# W

What's In It For Me? (WIIFM?) 33-34
Win/Win relationship 31, 80
Work-in-process 130, 142